# AAT

AF622669

Level 3

Diploma in Accounting

# Tax Processes for Businesses

## Course Book

For assessments from 26th January 2026 to 24th January 2027

BPP

Fourth edition

ISBN 9781 0355 3010 6

Previous ISBN 9781 0355 3010 6

ISBN (for internal use only) 9781 0355 2994 0

eISBN 9781 0355 3026 7

**British Library Cataloguing-in-Publication Data**

A catalogue record for this book is available from the British Library

**Published by**

BPP Learning Media Ltd
BPP House, Aldine Place
142–144 Uxbridge Road
London W12 8AA

learningmedia.bpp.com

Your learning materials are printed on paper obtained from traceable sustainable sources.

# Contents

# Introduction to the course

## Syllabus overview

This unit explores tax processes that influence the daily operations of businesses and is designed to develop students' skills in understanding, preparing, and submitting Value Added Tax (VAT) returns to HM Revenue and Customs (HMRC). The unit provides students with the knowledge and skills that are needed to keep businesses, employers and clients compliant with laws and practices that apply to VAT and payroll. Students will learn about legislation and the importance of maintaining their technical knowledge through monitoring updates.

### Test specification for this unit assessment

| Assessment method | Marking type | Duration of assessment |
|---|---|---|
| **Computer-based assessment** | **Computer marked** | 1.5 hours |

| Learning outcomes | Weighting |
|---|---|
| 1 Understand legislation requirements relating to VAT | 25% |
| 2 Calculate VAT | 30% |
| 3 Review and verify VAT returns | 20% |
| 4 Understand principles of payroll | 15% |
| 5 Report information within the organisation | 10% |
| **Total** | **100%** |

### Assessment structure

1½ hours duration

Competency is 70%

*Note that this is only a guideline as to what might come up. The format and content of each task may vary from what we have listed below.

Your assessment will consist of 8 tasks:

| Task | Expected content | Max marks | Chapter ref | Study complete |
|---|---|---|---|---|
| Task 1 | Understanding and calculating UK tax law principles relating to VAT, registration and deregistration and special schemes. | 9 | 1, 2, 6 | |
| Task 2 | Calculating and accounting for VAT – eg VAT calculations, invoices, discounts, and tax points. | 8 | 2,3,4 | |
| Task 3 | Input VAT recovery eg partial exemption, blocked input VAT, bad debts, discounts, and fuel scale charge. | 12 | 3,4 | |
| Task 4 | Preparing, calculating and adjusting information for VAT returns | 8 | 5, 8 | |

| Task | Expected content | Max marks | Chapter ref | Study complete |
|---|---|---|---|---|
| Task 5 | Verifying VAT returns | 12 | 5 | |
| Task 6 | VAT rules on record keeping, filing and payment/repayment, including non-compliance implications | 11 | 8 | |
| Task 7 | Principles of payroll | 12 | 7 | |
| Task 8 | Reporting information on VAT and payroll | 8 | 7,8 | |

## Skills bank

Our experience of preparing students for this type of assessment suggests that to obtain competency, you will need to develop a number of key skills.

**1** Learning and applying the theory

**2** Logical approaches to tasks

**3** Effective use of your time in the assessment

### What do I need to know to do well in the assessment?

*Tax Processes for Businesses* is designed to develop your skills in preparing VAT and payroll information to be provided to the relevant tax authority in situations where the transactions that have to be included are relatively routine.

To be successful in the assessment you need to:

- Understand legislation requirements relating to VAT
- Calculate VAT
- Review and verify VAT returns
- Understand principles of payroll
- Report information within the organisation

### Assumed knowledge

There is no assumed knowledge for this unit.

### Assessment style

In the assessment you will complete tasks by:

(a) Entering narrative by selecting from drop down menus of narrative options known as **picklists**

(b) Using **drag and drop** menus to enter narrative

(c) Typing in numbers, known as **gapfill** entry

(d) Entering **ticks**

(e) Entering **dates** by selecting from a calendar

You must familiarise yourself with the style of the online questions and the AAT software before taking the assessment. As part of your revision, login to the **AAT website** and attempt their **online practice assessments**.

# Introduction to the assessment

The question practice you do will prepare you for the format of tasks you will see in the *Tax Processes for Businesses* assessment. It is also useful to familiarise yourself with the introductory information you may be given at the start of the assessment. For example:

You have **1 hour and 30 minutes** to complete this assessment.

- This assessment contains **8 tasks,** and you should attempt to complete **every** task.
- Each task is independent. You will not need to refer to your answers to previous tasks.
- The total number of marks for this assessment is 80.
- Read every task carefully to make sure you understand what is required.
- Where the date is relevant, it is given in the task data.
- Both minus signs and brackets can be used to indicate negative numbers **unless** task instructions state otherwise.
- You must use a full stop to indicate a decimal point. For example, write 100.57 **not** 100,57 or 10057.
- You may use a comma to indicate a number in the thousands, but you don't have to. For example, 10000 and 10,000 are both acceptable.

(a) As you revise, use the **BPP Passcards** to consolidate your knowledge. They are a pocket-sized revision tool, perfect for packing in that last-minute revision.

(b) Attempt as many tasks as possible in the **Exam Practice Kit**. There are plenty of assessment-style tasks which are excellent preparation for the real assessment.

(c) Always **check** through your own answers as you will in the real assessment, before looking at the solutions in the back of the Exam Practice Kit.

# Key to icons

**Key term**

A key definition which is important to be aware of for the assessment.

**Formula to learn**

A formula you will need to learn as it will not be provided in the assessment.

**Formula provided**

A formula which is provided within the assessment and generally available as a pop-up on screen.

**Activity**

An example which allows you to apply your knowledge to the technique covered in the Course Book. The solution is provided at the end of the chapter.

**Illustration**

A worked example which can be used to review and see how an assessment question could be answered.

**Assessment focus point**

A high priority point for the assessment.

**Open book reference**

Where use of an open book will be allowed for the assessment.

**Real life examples**

A practical real life scenario.

## AAT qualifications

The material in this book may support the following AAT qualifications:

AAT Diploma in Accounting Level 3, AAT Level 3 Certificate in Bookkeeping and AAT Diploma in Accounting at SCQF Level 7.

### Supplements

From time to time we may need to publish supplementary materials to one of our titles. This can be for a variety of reasons, from a small change in the AAT unit guidance to new legislation coming into effect between editions.

**You should check our supplements page regularly** for anything that may affect your learning materials. All supplements are available free of charge on our supplements page on our website at:

learningmedia.bpp.com/pages/resources-for-students

### Improving material and removing errors

BPP Learning Media do everything possible to ensure the material is accurate and up to date when sending to print. In the event that any errors are found after the print date, they are uploaded to the following website: learningmedia.bpp.com/pages/errata

These learning materials are based on the qualification specification released by the AAT in July 2025.

## AAT Practice Assessment

The AAT practice assessments mimic the real exam and so must be attempted prior to taking the real exam. You should attempt these using a laptop/desktop computer, as this will give you a better feel for the actual AAT exam conditions.

Please note, at the end of each test you will be presented with feedback which you should review.

Use this link below to access the assessment required: https://www.aat.org.uk/learning-portal.

# 1 Introduction to VAT

## Learning outcomes

Having studied this chapter you will be able to:

| | |
|---|---|
| 1.1 | **UK tax law principles relating to VAT**<br>• Understand that HMRC is the relevant tax authority for VAT in the UK<br>• Understand that VAT is a tax on consumer spending, charged on taxable supplies by taxable persons, including whether the tax charged falls on registered businesses or the end user |
| 2.3 | **VAT calculations**<br>• Understand the difference between inputs and outputs, and between input tax and output tax |

## Assessment context

An awareness of how the VAT system works within the UK.

Includes important terminology which is used throughout the course.

## Qualification and Business context

It is the responsibility of the business to collect VAT on behalf of HMRC. As an accountant, you should be aware of how this process works.

## Chapter overview

**Introduction to VAT**

- **HMRC**
  - The relevant tax authority for VAT in the UK
- **Business**
  - A registered business collects VAT on behalf of HMRC
  - Charges output tax to customers
  - Reclaims input tax suffered on purchases
  - Net of output tax less input tax = VAT liability payable to HMRC
  - Liability declared to HMRC via VAT return
- **Customer**
  - Ultimately suffers all VAT because they cannot reclaim the input tax paid on purchases

# Introduction

Value Added Tax (VAT) is an indirect tax which is essentially a sales tax – it is a tax on consumer expenditure and is an important source of revenue for the government. The basic principle is that VAT should normally be borne by the final consumer but is collected at each stage of the value added process.

A VAT-registered trader will collect VAT by charging their customers VAT on sales (**output VAT**), and reclaim VAT they have suffered on their purchases (**input VAT**).

KEY TERM

**Output VAT :** VAT charged on the sale of goods and the provision of services by VAT-registered traders, which is paid by the business to HMRC

**Input VAT:** VAT on the purchase of goods and payment of expenses, which is reclaimed by the business from HMRC

A VAT-registered trader must digitally file a VAT return which states how much VAT is payable to His Majesty's Revenue and Customs (HMRC). The amount payable is the difference between the output VAT and the input VAT. HMRC is the government department charged with the administration and collection of taxes.

The current rate of VAT is **20%**.

## 1 Role of a business

The business that is registered for VAT acts as an agent for HMRC, collecting VAT on their behalf. If the business adds value, it will owe output VAT to HMRC and that makes VAT a liability in the books of the business.

Businesses have to make sure they account for VAT accurately; otherwise they could face penalties.

## 2 Collection of VAT

It is the end consumer (normally the general public) who suffers the full amount of VAT. However, the VAT is collected by HMRC at each value added stage of the production process.

### Illustration 1: Collection of VAT

| | Net sale price | Net purchase price | VAT (@ 20%) |
|---|---|---|---|
| | £ | £ | £ |
| Producer sells raw materials for £100.00 + VAT | 100.00 | | 20.00 |
| Total payable by producer to HMRC | | | 20.00 |
| Factory buys the raw materials to manufacture their product. They then sell this product to a retailer for £300.00 + VAT | | (100.00) | (20.00) |
| | 300.00 | | 60.00 |
| Total payable by factory to HMRC | | | 40.00 |
| Retailer buys the product and sells it on to the end customer for £360.00 + VAT | | (300.00) | (60.00) |
| | 360.00 | | 72.00 |
| Total payable by retailer to HMRC | | | 12.00 |

| ***VAT paid to HMRC at each stage of the value added process is:*** | **£** |
|---|---|
| Producer | 20.00 |
| Factory | 40.00 |
| Retailer | 12.00 |
| **Total** | 72.00 |
| | |
| **VAT suffered by end customer (who cannot reclaim) is:** | 72.00 |

## Activity 1: Input and output tax

Business A sells goods to Business B for £1,000 plus £200 of VAT.

**Required**

**Which business treats the VAT as input tax and which treats it as output tax?**

| | Input tax ✓ | Output tax ✓ |
|---|---|---|
| Business A | | |
| Business B | | |

## Chapter summary

- VAT is an indirect tax administered by HMRC.
- A purchaser who is not VAT-registered bears the cost of the VAT. This is normally the final purchaser in the supply chain, who is often a member of the public.

## Activity answers

### Activity 1: Input and output tax

The correct answers are:

| | Input tax ✓ | Output tax ✓ |
|---|---|---|
| Business A | | ✓ |
| Business B | ✓ | |

## Test your learning

1 **Which organisation administers VAT in the UK? Tick the relevant box below.**

| | |
|---|---|
| HM Customs & Excise | |
| Inland Revenue | |
| HM Revenue & Customs | |
| HM Treasury | |

2 **Choose which ONE of the following statements is correct. Tick the relevant box below.**

| | |
|---|---|
| Output VAT is the VAT charged by a supplier on the sales that are made by their business. Output VAT is collected by the supplier and paid over to HMRC. | |
| Output VAT is the VAT suffered by the purchaser of the goods which will be reclaimed from HMRC if the purchaser is VAT-registered. | |

3 **Explain how it is normally the final consumer that pays the full amount of VAT to the seller but never pays any money to HMRC.**

# 2 VAT basics

## Learning outcomes

This chapter addresses the following syllabus learning objectives:

| | |
|---|---|
| 1.2 | **VAT registration and deregistration requirements**<br>Learners need to understand:<br>• The registration and deregistration thresholds for the normal VAT scheme, and how to apply them<br>• The circumstances:<br>- in which voluntary registration may be beneficial to a business<br>- for voluntary and compulsory deregistration<br>• What is meant by the historic turnover method (historic test) and the future turnover method (future test), and how to comply with them in respect of registration<br>• The definitions of:<br>- taxable supplies<br>- standard-rated supplies<br>- reduced-rated supplies<br>- zero-rated supplies<br>- exempt supplies<br>- supplies outside the scope of VAT |
| 2.3 | **VAT calculations**<br>• Understand the different implications of exempt supplies and of zero-rated supplies, and the effect on recovery of input tax |

## Assessment context

Task 1 in the exam may ask you to identify when a taxable trader needs to register for VAT and also what the impact of this will be on the business.

Task 3 in the exam may ask you about exempt supplies and the difference between a zero-rated supplier and an exempt supplier. There is no knowledge required of the detail of which specific items fall into each category of supply.

## Qualification and Business context

Understand that not all businesses will need to be VAT-registered. However, if they are registered, you will need to know what the impact of this is.

## Business context

You will need to have an awareness that there are different rates of VAT for different types of product.

The benefits of registering for VAT are abundant to a business, but consideration must be given to potential drawbacks.

## Chapter overview

**VAT basics**

**Scope of VAT**

**Taxable supplies**

- Taxable supplies are at standard rate (20%), reduced rate (5%) or zero rated (0%)
- Taxable persons making taxable supplies can recover input VAT on business purchases

**Exempt supplies**

- Exempt suppliers not permitted to register for VAT
- No VAT on sales
- Exempt traders cannot recover any input tax (all costs gross in accounts)

**Registration**

**Compulsory**

- Past (historic) turnover exceeds registration threshold in previous 12 months (cumulative)
- Future turnover will exceed registration threshold in next 30 days alone
- Deregistration compulsory if cease to make taxable supplies, voluntary if taxable supplies fall under deregistration threshold

**Voluntary**

- Advantages: recover input tax, avoid penalties for late registration, business looks more substantial
- Disadvantages: obligation to file VAT returns, keep records, issue VAT invoices, exposure to penalties for errors and late filing, prices increase if customers cannot reclaim VAT

## Introduction

For VAT purposes, supplies are classified as either taxable (standard-rated (20%), reduced-rated (5%) or zero-rated (0%)), exempt, or outside the scope of VAT. It is important to note carefully which category a supply falls into as it will determine the rate of output tax charged to the customer, and whether the business can recover related input tax suffered.

Once a business's taxable supplies have reached a certain level, the business is required to register for VAT. This is known as compulsory registration. It is also possible to voluntarily register for VAT. A business may deregister for VAT if its supplies fall below a certain threshold, but it must deregister if it ceases to make any taxable supplies.

# 1 Scope of VAT

VAT is chargeable on **taxable supplies** of goods and services made in the UK by **taxable persons** in the course of their business.

A **taxable person** is an individual or company who is required to register for VAT (see registration below).

KEY TERM

**Taxable supplies:** Taxable supplies are those which are:

- Standard-rated (20%)
- Zero-rated (0%)
- Reduced-rated (5%)

**Standard-rated supplies:** Goods and services which are taxable at a rate of 20%.

**Zero-rated supplies:** Goods and services which are taxable, but the rate of tax on them is 0%, for example non-luxury food, children's clothing

**Reduced-rated supplies:** Goods and services which are taxable at a rate of 5%, for example domestic fuel

**Exempt supplies:** For example, insurance or postal services, are not taxable supplies, so no VAT is charged.

**Supplies outside the scope of VAT:** For example, wages; these are outside the UK VAT system altogether and have no impact on VAT calculations.

You will be told in the exam if a supply is taxable and, if so, at which rate.

A supplier making solely taxable supplies may, or in certain circumstances must, register for VAT and can then recover the input tax suffered on their purchases.

If a supplier only makes exempt supplies, then they cannot register for VAT and will not be able to recover input tax suffered on their purchases.

### Illustration 1: Calculation of VAT payable

| | Type of supplies | | |
|---|---|---|---|
| | Standard-rated | Zero-rated | Exempt |
| | £ | £ | £ |
| Supplies (net) | 30,000 | 30,000 | 30,000 |
| VAT charged on supplies | 6,000 | 0 | n/a |
| | 36,000 | 30,000 | 30,000 |
| Purchases (net) | 20,000 | 20,000 | 20,000 |

| | Type of supplies | | |
|---|---|---|---|
| | Standard-rated | Zero-rated | Exempt |
| | £ | £ | £ |
| VAT charged on purchases (all purchases are standard-rated) | 4,000 | 4,000 | 4,000 |
| | 24,000 | 24,000 | 24,000 |
| VAT payable/(reclaimable) | 2,000 | (4,000) | Nil |

## 1.1 Cost to the business

- As businesses making taxable supplies that are registered for VAT can reclaim the input tax paid on their purchases and expenses, the cost to the business is the VAT-exclusive ("net") amount.
- As businesses making only exempt supplies cannot register for VAT and therefore cannot reclaim the input tax paid on their purchases and expenses, the cost to the business is the VAT-inclusive ("gross") amount.

### Activity 1: Cost to business

The following businesses have just paid telephone bills of £1,200 (£1,000 plus VAT of £200).

**Required**

**What is the net cost incurred by each business in relation to the telephone bills?**

| Business type | Type of supply made | Net cost £ |
|---|---|---|
| Insurance company | Only exempt supplies | |
| Accountancy firm | Only standard-rated supplies | |
| Bus company | Only zero-rated supplies | |

# 2 Registration

KEY TERM

**Registration:** The process required if a business making taxable supplies must (if it exceeds the registration limits), or wants to, start charging (and recovering) VAT. VAT must be charged on taxable supplies from the date of registration.

## 2.1 Compulsory registration

**Registration** is compulsory if a taxable person meets one of the following two tests:

(a) **Historic turnover method ('historic test')**

Check at the end of each month if the total taxable turnover over the previous 12 months exceeds the registration limit of £90,000.

For a new business the period may be shorter, ie from the start of trade to the current month end. It must not, however, exceed 12 months.

(b) **Future turnover method ('future test')**

Each day check if the total taxable turnover over for just the next 30 days alone is likely to exceed the registration limit of £90,000.

If either test is passed, the taxable person must notify HMRC within 30 days of the date of the historic test, and before the end of the 30-day period the future test.

Registration is effective from:

(a) Start of month following the end of the 30-day notification period (historic test).

(b) Start of the 30-day period (future test).

KEY TERM

**Taxable turnover:** The VAT-exclusive value of all zero-rated, reduced-rated and standard-rated supplies. Exempt sales are excluded.

## Illustration 2: Historic test

Jack started his business on 1 July 2025. His monthly VAT-exclusive turnover is:

| | £ |
|---|---|
| Standard-rated supplies | 8,000 |
| Zero-rated supplies | 2,850 |
| Exempt supplies | 600 |
| Total | 11,450 |

**Required**

**(a) Calculate the VAT-exclusive taxable turnover for each month (standard plus zero-rated supplies). Exclude the exempt supplies.**

**(b) Work out when the £90,000 registration limit is exceeded (if at all), up to a maximum of a 12-month period.**

**Solution**

**(a)** Taxable turnover is £10,850 per month (£8,000 + £2,850).

**(b)** After eight months (28 February 2026) cumulative turnover is £86,800, so the limit is not exceeded.

After nine months (31 March 2026) cumulative turnover is £97,650 so the limit is exceeded.

Therefore, after nine months Jack must register for VAT within 30 days (ie by 30 April 2026). His registration will be effective from 1 May 2026.

## Illustration 3: Future test

Orla has been in business for many years with VAT-exclusive turnover of approximately £7,250 per month (£87,000 per annum) and so has not yet had to register under the historic test. On 24 November 2025, Orla won a major contract which will immediately bring in additional income of approximately £82,800 per month.

Taxable turnover in the next 30 days alone will be £90,050 (£7,250 + £82,800), which exceeds the threshold, therefore Orla must register for VAT by 24 December 2025, and her registration will be effective (ie she needs to charge VAT to her customers) immediately.

## Activity 2: Mark – Registration

Mark commenced trading as a carpenter on 1 October 2025. He makes only taxable supplies. The turnover (net of VAT) for each quarter has been shown below. Turnover is spread evenly over the quarter.

| Quarter ended | Turnover £ |
|---|---|
| 31 December 2025 | 19,500 |
| 31 March 2026 | 21,750 |
| 30 June 2026 | 22,800 |
| 30 September 2026 | 24,000 |
| 31 December 2026 | 25,500 |
| 31 March 2027 | 17,000 |

**Required**

**(a) When will Mark breach one of the registration tests?**

**(b) By what date is he required to notify HMRC that he is liable to register for VAT?**

**(c) When will Mark be registered for VAT?**

## Activity 3: Registration scenarios

You have the following information about the taxable supplies of three businesses.

**Required**

**For each of them, indicate whether they need to register for VAT immediately, or monitor turnover and register later. Tick ONE box on EACH line.**

| | Register now ✓ | Monitor and register later ✓ |
|---|---|---|
| A new business with an expected turnover of £8,000 per month for the next 12 months. | | |

|  | Register now ✓ | Monitor and register later ✓ |
|---|---|---|
| An existing business with a total turnover of £79,000 for the last 11 months. Sales for the next 30 days are not yet known. |  |  |
| An existing business with a total turnover of £8,000 per month for the last 12 months. |  |  |

## 2.2 Exemptions from compulsory registration

The registration requirement can be waived under two circumstances:

(a) If the business can satisfy HMRC that taxable supplies in the following 12month period will be less than the deregistration threshold of £88,000.

(b) If the business makes only (or mainly) zero-rated supplies.

**Registration decision tree**

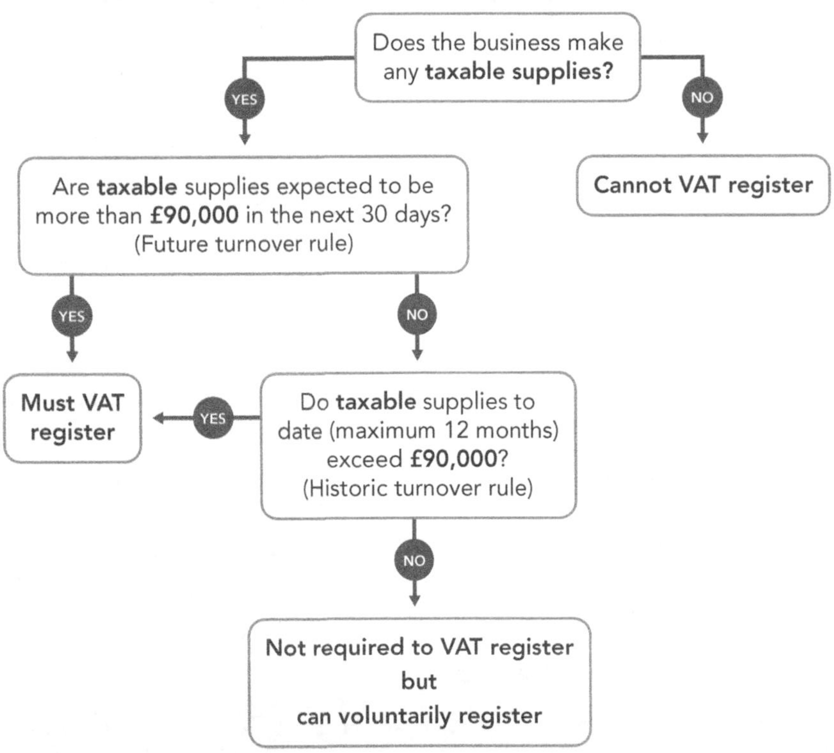


## 2.3 Voluntary registration

A business may apply for VAT registration even though its taxable turnover is below the registration threshold.

Zero-rated traders may choose to register early to produce a net repayment position.

## 2.4 Implications of registration

Some benefits and drawbacks of registration are highlighted below:

| Advantages | Disadvantages |
|---|---|
| • Recover input tax | • Administration burden |
| • Discipline | • Risk of penalties on errors |
| • Avoid late registration penalty | • Prices go up for non-VAT-registered customers as they cannot reclaim the input tax on the purchase (need to look at customer status) |
| • A small business may appear to be more established/credible | |

### Activity 4: Voluntary registration

**Choose ONE reason why a business making taxable supplies might choose not to register for VAT voluntarily.**

| | ✓ |
|---|---|
| Preparation of VAT returns would be required. | |
| Customers would benefit by being able to claim back input tax. | |
| The business would benefit by being able to claim back input tax. | |

## 2.5 Deregistration

If the business ceases to make taxable supplies, it **must deregister**. The business must inform HMRC within 30 days of ceasing to make taxable supplies.

A business may **voluntarily** deregister if in the next 12-month period the VAT-exclusive value of taxable supplies will be below £88,000.

## 2.6 Failure to register

If the business fails to register on time, it will be taxed as if it had registered on time. The business will therefore still owe to HMRC the VAT that it should have been collecting on sales since the date on which registration should have been effective.

The business can calculate this in two ways:

(a) Treat its sales as VAT inclusive and pay the VAT out of profits.

(b) Treat its sales as VAT exclusive and try to get the extra money owed for the VAT from its customers.

The failure of a business to register for VAT may also incur a penalty in addition to the tax payable (see Chapter 8).

## Chapter summary

- There are two types of supply – taxable supplies and exempt supplies.
- In the UK there are three rates of VAT for taxable supplies – the standard rate of 20%, a reduced rate of 5% for certain supplies such as domestic fuel and power, and the zero rate.
- In a VAT-registered business, VAT does not increase the selling prices of either zero-rated supplies or exempt supplies. However, if a business makes exempt supplies, it cannot reclaim the input tax on its purchases and expenses. If the supplies made by the business are zero-rated, then input tax can be reclaimed.
- The cost of purchases to a VAT-registered business making taxable supplies is generally the VAT-exclusive price. The cost of purchases to a business not registered for VAT, including a business making wholly exempt supplies, is the VAT-inclusive price.
- When a business's taxable turnover reaches the registration limit, the business must register for VAT; otherwise the business is liable for penalties (see Chapter 8).
- Some businesses may find it advantageous to register for VAT even though the registration limit has not been met – this is known as voluntary registration.
- If a business's taxable turnover falls below the deregistration limit, then the business can apply to HMRC to deregister.
- If a business ceases to make taxable supplies, then it must deregister.

# Activity answers

### Activity 1: Cost to business

| Business type | Type of supply made | Net cost<br>£ |
|---|---|---|
| Insurance company | Only exempt supplies | 1,200 |
| Accountancy firm | Only standard-rated supplies | 1,000 |
| Bus company | Only zero-rated supplies | 1,000 |

Although the accountancy firm and bus company pay £1,200 for their telephone bills, they are able to reclaim the input tax of £200, so the net cost is £1,000. The insurance company making exempt supplies is not able to reclaim input tax and so the net cost is £1,200.

### Activity 2: Mark – Registration

**(a)** As his turnover in the last 12 months does not exceed £90,000 until 31 October 2026 (on a month-by-month basis) he does not become liable until then.

*Working*

12 months to 30 September = £88,050

12 months to 31 October = £88,050 + (£25,500/3) – (£19,500/3) = £90,050

**(b)** He must then notify HMRC within 30 days, ie by 30 November 2026.

**(c)** He is then registered from 1 December 2026 or an earlier date by mutual agreement.

### Activity 3: Registration scenarios

The correct answers are:

| | Register now<br>✓ | Monitor and register later<br>✓ |
|---|---|---|
| A new business with an expected turnover of £8,000 per month for the next 12 months. | | ✓ |
| An existing business with a total turnover of £79,000 for the last 11 months. Sales for the next 30 days are not yet known. | | ✓ |
| An existing business with a total turnover of £8,000 per month for the last 12 months. | ✓ | |

*Working*

(1) Monitor and register later, as neither the historic nor the future test have been exceeded at this point

(2) Monitor and register later, as taxable supplies have not yet exceeded £90,000 in the last 12 months

(3) Register now, as taxable supplies in the previous 12 months exceed £90,000

### Activity 4: Voluntary registration

The correct answer is:

| | ✓ |
|---|---|
| Preparation of VAT returns would be required. | ✓ |
| Customers would benefit by being able to claim back input tax. | |
| The business would benefit by being able to claim back input tax. | |

Option C is factually correct; but VAT can only be claimed back once registered. Option B is not correct because VAT-registered customers would neither gain nor lose because they could reclaim VAT charged to them, and non-registered customers would be disadvantaged because they would be charged VAT they could not reclaim.

## Test your learning

1 **Identify whether the following statements are true or false.**

| | True ✓ | False ✓ |
|---|---|---|
| If a business supplies zero-rated services, then the business is not able to reclaim the VAT on its purchases and expenses from HMRC. | | |
| A business makes zero-rated supplies. The cost to the business of its purchases and expenses is the VAT-exclusive amount. | | |

2 You have been contacted by a potential new client, Mrs Quirke. She has recently started trading as an interior designer.

**Required**

**By selecting from the options listed, complete the following letter to her, explaining when her business must register for VAT.**

AN Accountant

Number Street

London

SW11 8AB

Mrs Quirke

Alphabet Street

London

W12 6WM

Dear Mrs Quirke

VAT REGISTRATION

Further to our recent telephone conversation, set out below are the circumstances when you must register your business for VAT.

If the taxable turnover of your business at the end of a month, looking back no more than (1) ▼ months, has exceeded the registration limit of (2) ▼, then the business must apply to register for VAT within 30 days.

Alternatively, if at any time, the taxable turnover (before any VAT is added) is expected to exceed the registration limit within the next (3) ▼ alone, then the business must apply to be registered for VAT without delay. This would be the situation if, for example, you obtained a large additional contract for, say, £92,000.

If you wish to discuss this in any more detail, please do not hesitate to contact me.

Yours sincerely

AN Accountant

**Picklist 1**

- 12
- 24
- 6

**Picklist 2**

- £83,000
- £85,000
- £90,000

**Picklist 3**

- 12 months
- 30 days
- Week

3 Amy started trading on 1 August 2025. Her monthly sales (excluding VAT) are:

| | £ |
|---|---|
| Standard-rated supplies | 7,850 |
| Zero-rated supplies | 2,210 |
| Exempt supplies | 700 |
| | 10,760 |

**Required**

By what date will Amy exceed the threshold for VAT? ☐

By what date must Amy register for VAT? ☐

4 Richard made taxable supplies of £79,500 in his first 11 months of trading. His taxable supplies in month 12 are £11,000.

**Required**

**Which of the following explains why Richard must register for VAT? Tick ONE box.**

| | |
|---|---|
| At the beginning of month 12, Richard expects his taxable supplies to exceed £90,000 in the next 30 days. | |
| At the end of month 12, Richard's taxable supplies in the previous 12 months will have exceeded £90,000. | |

5 **Decide why a business making taxable supplies might choose to register for VAT voluntarily. Tick ONE box.**

| | |
|---|---|
| Preparation of VAT returns would be optional. | |
| Customers would benefit by being able to claim back input tax. | |
| It is a new business and wishes to appear larger or more established. | |

6 Freya is not registered for VAT. Her supplies are £6,000 per month. On 10/04/20X5 she has a new customer who will order £92,000 of goods from her on 30/04/20X5.

**Required**

**Freya must notify HMRC that she is liable to register for VAT by** [ ] **and her registration will take effect on** [ ▼ ] .

# 3 Inputs and outputs

## Learning outcomes

| | |
|---|---|
| 2.3 | **VAT calculations**<br>• Calculate VAT when given the net or gross amount of the supply<br>• Understand rounding rules on VAT calculations<br>• Calculate VAT on standard-rated supplies and reduced-rated supplies<br>• Understand the identification of what cannot be claimed as input tax: expenditure on employee and business contact entertaining, including that of mixed groups; purchases and sales of cars and vans; and assets with private use<br>• Understand the VAT rules on fuel scale charges, how to apply them and their effect on VAT payable or reclaimable<br>• Calculate the impact on VAT of fuel scale charges; and items on which input tax cannot be reclaimed<br>• Understand how partial exemption works, the *deminimis* limit and how this affects the recovery of input tax<br>• Calculate VAT for international trade: imports and exports<br>• Understand how to account for postponed import tax |
| 3.2 | **Verify information contained within VAT returns**<br>• Understand how imports and exports are treated on a VAT return |

## Assessment context

Calculating and interpreting VAT is core to this unit. You will need to know how VAT is affected by different types of transactions. There is lots of information available in the reference material which will be available during the exam.

Task 2 will examine detailed VAT calculations. Task 3 may test your understanding of partial exemption rules and irrecoverable input tax.

## Qualification context

You should be aware of the fact that the calculation of VAT changes depending on the type of transaction.

## Business context

Every registered business needs to account for VAT accurately using the rules set out by the VAT legislation. These rules are some of the basics that you will need to be aware of in business.

## Chapter overview

**Inputs and Outputs**

**Calculation of VAT**

- Price given inclusive of VAT:
  - × 20/120 if standard-rated
  - × 5/105 if reduced-rated
- Price given exclusive of VAT: × 20% or 5% to get VAT
- VAT usually rounded down to nearest 1p
- VAT liability = output tax – recoverable input tax for the period

**Irrecoverable input tax**

- Cannot recover input tax on:
  - UK Business entertaining
  - Cars
  - Private use items
- VAT on private fuel is recoverable but add fuel scale charge to output tax

**Partially exempt traders**

- Make taxable and exempt supplies (only charge VAT on taxable supplies)
- Must attribute or apportion input tax between taxable and exempt supplies
- Input tax re exempt supplies is recoverable if meet de minimis test

**Overseas transactions**

- Imports – pay input tax at border or via postponed accounting. Recover as per usual rules
- Exports – always zero rated if proof of export
- Service supplied overseas – charge UK VAT if BTC
- Service purchased from overseas – reverse charge input tax as for postponed accounting

# Introduction

VAT is calculated as a percentage of the value of the supply. As we saw in the previous chapter, the rate of VAT may be 20%, 5% or 0%. In the exam, you may need to calculate VAT when given either the net (VAT exclusive), or gross (VAT inclusive) value of the supply, so it is important to read the detail of the question carefully.

One of the main advantages to being a VAT-registered business is the ability to recover VAT suffered on purchases. However, there are certain items that are blocked that you need to be aware of. There are also special rules for fuel purchases where there is some private use.

Where a business makes a mixture of supplies that includes both taxable and exempt supplies, the general rule if that it can only recover input tax that relates to the taxable supplies, and we have a set of rules to work out the proportion of input tax that relates to taxable supplies. However, where the input tax that relates to exempt supplies is below a certain level (de minimis), it can in fact be recovered.

Where a business sells goods to an overseas customer (export), or purchases goods from an overseas supplier (import), there are a specific set of rules to determine how VAT is charged or recovered. There are different rules where services are supplied or received from overseas.

# 1 Calculating VAT

VAT charged on taxable supplies is based on the VAT-exclusive value.

Prices given to you by the examiner can be either inclusive (gross) or exclusive (net) of VAT. (You will always be told which is the case.)

### Formula to learn

If an invoice shows that a standard-rated supply (VAT at 20%) has a **VAT-exclusive** amount of £100.00 then the VAT is calculated as:

£100.00 × 20% = £20.00

If an invoice shows that a standard-rated supply has a **VAT-inclusive** amount of £120.00, the amount of VAT can be calculated in one of two ways:

Either:

£120.00 × 20/120 = £20.00, or

£120.00 × 1/6 = £20.00

| Type of supply | Apply to 'net' value (VAT exclusive) | Apply to 'gross' value (VAT inclusive) |
|---|---|---|
| Standard-rated supply | 20% | 1/6 (20/120) |
| Reduced-rated supply | 5% | 5/105 |

### Illustration 1: Calculation of VAT

An invoice shows a total VAT-inclusive (gross) amount of £48.00. The amount of VAT at 20% included in this amount can be calculated as follows:

£48.00 × 20/120 = £8.00

or

£48.00 × 1/6 = £8.00

You can check this working by applying the 20% to the VAT-exclusive (net) amount:

£48.00 less £8.00 (VAT worked out above) = £40.00 (net amount)

£40.00 × 20% = £8.00

### Activity 1: Calculation of VAT – Inclusive price

VAT-inclusive price = £642.00 (standard rate @ 20%).

**Required**

**Calculate the VAT.**

## 1.1 Rounding of VAT

Any VAT calculation should normally be rounded down to the nearest penny. (This concession is not available to retailers.)

### Activity 2: Calculation of VAT – Rounding

An item has a net value of £54.89.

**Required**

**How much VAT (@ 20%) should be charged on this item?**

## 1.2 VAT payable to HMRC

Each VAT period (see Chapter 5) a taxable person will need to calculate how much VAT is owed to/repayable from HMRC.

| This is calculated as: | £ |
|---|---|
| Output tax | X |
| Less: | |
| Input tax | (X) |
| VAT payable/(repayable) | X/(X) |



BPP

### Activity 3: Calculation of VAT – VAT payable

A business buys goods for £1,000 excluding 20% VAT. It then sells those goods for £1,800 inclusive of 20% VAT.

**Required**

**What is the total VAT paid to or reclaimed from the HMRC?**

| | ✓ |
|---|---|
| £200 paid | |
| £300 reclaimed | |
| £100 paid | |
| £100 reclaimed | |

---

Usually (when input tax is recoverable), the cost to a VAT-registered business of buying goods and services is the **VAT-exclusive (net) amount**. For example:

| | £ |
|---|---|
| Amount paid to supplier (VAT inclusive) | 1,200 |
| Input tax reclaimed from HMRC | (200) |
| Net cost to the business (VAT exclusive) | 1,000 |

However, in certain circumstances, a business may not be able to recover all the input tax it has incurred on its purchases. Where VAT is irrecoverable, the cost to the business is the **VAT-inclusive amount.**

# 2 Irrecoverable input tax

If a taxable person (one who is making taxable supplies – standard, reduced or zero-rated) is registered for VAT, then they will be able to recover their input tax. There are, however, some circumstances where input tax cannot be recovered.

## 2.1 Business entertaining

The input tax incurred on business entertaining is not recoverable from HMRC. Business entertaining, however, does not include the following:

(a) Staff entertaining.

(b) Entertaining of non-UK customers.

The recovery of input tax, where there is a mixed group of staff and non-staff being entertained, would be apportioned appropriately.

## 2.2 Cars and vans

Unless a car is used exclusively for business purposes, then none of the input tax, including the VAT on car accessories purchased at the same time, will be recoverable. (There will be no output tax charged on disposal either as this will be an exempt supply.)

There are some exceptions to this, for example cars used:

- Exclusively for business purposes (eg pool cars)
- Within a taxi business
- For driving instruction
- Within a self-drive hire business

In the assessment, you will need to assume that the car has some private use unless told otherwise.

When purchasing a van, as long as the van is used at least partly to make taxable supplies, then the input tax will be recoverable. For this reason, when the van is sold, output tax would need to be charged on disposal.

| Capital item | Input tax recoverable on purchase? | Output tax chargeable on sale of item? |
|---|---|---|
| New car for employee's use | NO | NO – Exempt |
| Car used in taxi business | YES | YES |
| Van | YES | YES |

### Activity 4: Reclaiming input tax

**Identify whether input tax can be reclaimed by a VAT-registered business in each of the following circumstances.**

| Circumstance | Yes, can reclaim ✓ | No, cannot reclaim ✓ |
|---|---|---|
| Input tax incurred on entertaining prospective new UK client | | |
| Input tax incurred on a new car for the top salesperson | | |
| Input tax incurred on a car for use in a driving instruction business | | |

## 2.3 Private use

If an item purchased is being used for business and private purposes, then the portion of input tax relating to the private use would not be recoverable.

## 2.4 Fuel for private use

Input tax on all road fuel purchased by the business and used for business purposes can be reclaimed.

However, when a taxable person purchases fuel and it is used for private motoring by an employee or the sole trader/partner, then this has an impact on the recoverability of the input tax. The taxable person has a number of options:

(a) Ensure that the individual keeps sufficient mileage records so that the input tax on just the business miles can be recovered.

(b) Reclaim all the input VAT suffered on fuel but then account for some **output tax** using a set **fuel scale charge** per quarter. This scale charge is based on the $CO_2$ emissions of the vehicle, and will be given to you in the exam if needed.

(c) Agree not to reclaim any input tax on fuel purchased for any (including commercial) vehicles.

KEY TERM

**Fuel scale charge:** An output tax charge to offset against the input tax reclaimed on fuel purchased for private use.

### Illustration 2: Fuel scale charge

Josie is an employee of SMH Ltd. She has the use of a car which is used for both business and private purposes during the current VAT quarter.

SMH Ltd pays all the petrol costs in respect of the car, totalling £1,200.00. SMH Ltd does not require Josie to keep accurate private mileage records. SMH Ltd wishes to reclaim the input tax incurred.

The relevant quarterly fuel scale charge for Josie's car is £578.

All figures are inclusive of VAT.

The effect of the above on the quarterly VAT return is:

SMH Ltd may reclaim all of the input tax on the fuel £1,200.00 × 1/6 = £200.00 but must pay output tax calculated on the fuel scale charge £578.00 × 1/6 = £96.33 (note that normal mathematic rounding rules apply).

### Activity 5: Reclaiming input tax on private fuel

**Decide whether each of the following statements is true or false.**

| | True ✓ | False ✓ |
|---|---|---|
| A VAT-registered business can reclaim all the input tax on road fuel if it keeps detailed records of business and private mileage, and makes no other adjustment. | | |
| A VAT-registered business can reclaim all the input VAT on road fuel if it pays the appropriate fuel scale charge for private mileage. | | |

## 3 Partially exempt traders

KEY TERM

> **Partially exempt traders:** When a business makes a mixture of taxable and exempt supplies, input tax attributable to exempt supplies may only be reclaimed subject to satisfying *de minimis* tests.

How much input tax a taxable person can reclaim is determined by the types of supplies they make, as discussed in Chapter 2 of this Course Book.

A taxable trader making only taxable supplies (standard, reduced or zero-rated) can reclaim all their input tax, subject to the exceptions noted above.

An exempt trader, making only exempt supplies, cannot reclaim any of their input tax.

There are, however, some traders who make both taxable and exempt supplies. These are called **partially exempt traders**.

Partially exempt traders:

(a) Only charge output tax on their taxable supplies.

(b) Can reclaim the input tax on all purchases directly related to taxable supplies.

(c) Can reclaim a proportion of input tax which is not directly attributable to taxable or exempt supplies. This is based on the following calculation:

| | | | |
|---|---|---|---|
| Input tax not directly attributable to taxable or exempt supplies | × | Value of taxable supplies made / total supplies made | * |

*** round up to nearest per cent**

The rest of the input tax is only recoverable if it is below the **de *minimis* limit**: the amount is below £625 per month on average, **and** it is ≤ 50% of the total input tax for the period.

> ### Assessment focus point
>
> Note that your assessment will not test the detailed calculations. However, the following table should aid your understanding.

| Input tax | Recoverable | Not recoverable |
|---|---|---|
| Directly attributed to taxable supplies | ✔ | |
| Directly attributed to exempt supplies | | ✕ |

| Input tax | Recoverable | Not recoverable |
|---|---|---|
| Indirectly attributed (split using calculation) | ✔ | ✕<br>UNLESS<br>below *de minimis* limits |

## Activity 6: Partially exempt trader – Calculation

For the quarter ended 30 June 2025, Jim has allocated his input tax suffered between taxable and exempt supplies, but a balance remains unallocated.

| Exempt<br>£ | Taxable<br>£ | Unallocated<br>£ | Total input tax<br>£ |
|---|---|---|---|
| 700 | 20,000 | 3,000 | 23,700 |

His total turnover for the quarter was £135,429, of which taxable supplies amounted to £114,573.

**Required**

**How much of the £23,700 input tax suffered is recoverable by Jim?**

**Attributable to taxable supplies**

| | £ |
|---|---|
| Directly allocated | |
| **Indirectly allocated:** | |
| | |
| | |

**Attributable to exempt supplies**

| | £ |
|---|---|
| Directly allocated | |
| **Indirectly allocated:** | |
| | |
| | |

## Activity 7: Partially exempt trader – Multiple choice

A business supplies goods that are a mixture of standard-rated, exempt and zero-rated.

**Required**

**Which of the following statements is true? Choose ONE answer.**

| | ✓ |
|---|---|
| All of the input tax can be reclaimed. | |
| None of the input tax can be reclaimed. | |
| All of the input tax can be reclaimed, providing certain (de minimis) conditions are met. | |
| Some of the input tax can be reclaimed, in proportion to the different types of supply. | |

# 4 Overseas Transactions

Following the UK's exit from the EU, transactions between UK businesses and overseas customers and suppliers are all treated in the same way for VAT purposes, irrespective of whether the overseas customer or supplier is based in the EU or elsewhere.

**Assessment focus point**

Special rules still apply to transactions to/from Northern Ireland, however, these are not examinable in Tax Processes for Businesses.

## 4.1 Determining the place of supply

UK VAT is charged on supplies within the UK. It is therefore important to understand whether or not a supply is 'in the UK'. This is determined by the 'place of supply' rules.

**Goods** are deemed to be supplied where they 'originate', or start their journey. If they are located in the UK before being shipped to a customer, the place of supply is the UK.

**Services** are a little more complex. If the supply is to a registered business customer (eg, the performance of a company audit by its external auditors), they are deemed to be supplied where the customer is located. Other supplies of services (to non-registered businesses or consumers) are deemed to be supplied in the seller's country.

## 4.2 International transactions

**Exports**

**Goods** supplied to overseas customers are referred to as **exports** and are always zero-rated, provided the trader obtains evidence of their export within three months.

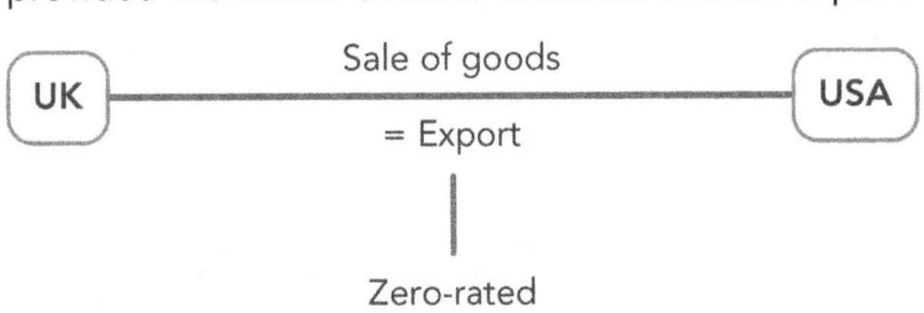


If **services** are exported, ie sold to overseas customers, UK VAT rules apply if the place of supply is the UK, so:

- If the service is being supplied to a non-business customer, the place of supply is the UK and the relevant UK rate of VAT will apply to the sale, and
- If the supply is being made to a business customer, the place of supply is not the UK, so UK VAT rules do not apply.

### Imports

**Goods** which are purchased from overseas countries are known as **imports**. No VAT is charged by the supplier. When the goods enter the UK, the purchaser needs to pay the applicable rate of UK VAT.

### Postponed accounting

When a UK business imports goods into the UK, it works out the UK VAT that would be payable on them if they had been bought from a UK supplier. This is import VAT. The import VAT is then included on the UK trader's next VAT return as both output tax and input tax, which makes the import VAT neutral for a taxable supplier. This practice is called postponed accounting.

Postponed accounting was introduced in January 2021. Prior to this a business which imported goods into the UK had to actually pay the import VAT on the goods at their point of entry into the UK in order to access the goods at customs. The UK importer would then recover that import VAT as input tax in their VAT return. This method is still possible but unless told otherwise in your assessment, you should assume that postponed accounting is being used as a default.

### Imports of services

The reverse charge system applies to all purchases of services from overseas suppliers by business customers – the UK business adds the applicable VAT to output tax on its VAT return.

### Recovery of input tax on imports

Irrespective of the method by which the import VAT is paid (at the border or via postponed accounting/reverse charge for services), the input tax paid can be recovered by the business according to usual rules.

## Activity 8: Postponed accounting

A UK VAT-registered trader purchases goods from a supplier in Australia. These goods would have been standard-rated if they were purchased in the UK.

**Required**

**Which of the following is a correct VAT treatment?**

| | ✓ |
|---|---|
| Australian VAT would have been applied by the seller so no UK VAT applies | |
| Imports of goods are always zero-rated | |
| The trader may charge UK VAT at 20% on the value of the imported goods as output tax on its next VAT return | |

## Chapter summary

- VAT is charged on standard-rated supplies at 20%. The VAT amount in a VAT-inclusive price is found by multiplying by 1/6.
- The VAT on business entertainment expenses of UK customers and (usually) on the purchase of cars for use within a business is non-reclaimable.
- If input tax is reclaimed on fuel used for private journeys, an amount of output tax (the fuel scale charge) also has to be charged.
- If a VAT-registered business makes both taxable and exempt supplies, it is partially exempt. The recovery of input tax will be restricted, subject to the *de minimis* limits.
- Exports of goods to another country are treated as zero-rated supplies.
- Exports of services only have UK VAT applied where they are made to non-business customers.
- Goods imported are charged at the same rate as goods purchased in the UK. The tax is added as both output tax and input tax on its next VAT return via the 'postponed accounting' system.
- VAT on imported services is added to output tax on the trader's next VAT return via the reverse charge system but can usually reclaim it as input VAT on same VAT return.

## Activity answers

### Activity 1: Calculation of VAT – Inclusive price

VAT = 642.00 × 1/6

= £107.00

### Activity 2: Calculation of VAT – Rounding

VAT = £54.89 × 20%

= £10.978

= £10.97 (rounded down to the nearest penny)

### Activity 3: Calculation of VAT – VAT payable

The correct answer is:

| | ✓ |
|---|---|
| £200 paid | |
| £300 reclaimed | |
| £100 paid | ✓ |
| £100 reclaimed | |

Output tax is payable of £300 less input tax recoverable of £200. The net amount of VAT to pay to HMRC is £100.

*Working*

| | £ |
|---|---|
| Output tax £1,800 × 1/6 | 300 |
| Input tax £1,000 × 20% | (200) |
| VAT payable | 100 |

### Activity 4: Reclaiming input tax

The correct answers are:

| Circumstance | Yes, can reclaim ✓ | No, cannot reclaim ✓ |
|---|---|---|
| Input tax incurred on entertaining prospective new UK client | | ✓ |
| Input tax incurred on a new car for the top salesperson | | ✓ |
| Input tax incurred on a car for use in a driving instruction business | ✓ | |

### Activity 5: Reclaiming input tax on private fuel

The correct answers are:

| | True ✓ | False ✓ |
|---|---|---|
| A VAT-registered business can reclaim all the input tax on road fuel if it keeps detailed records of business and private mileage, and makes no other adjustment. | | ✓ |
| A VAT-registered business can reclaim all the input VAT on road fuel if it pays the appropriate fuel scale charge for private mileage. | ✓ | |

### Activity 6: Partially exempt trader – Calculation

**Attributable to taxable supplies**

| | £ |
|---|---|
| Directly allocated | 20,000 |
| **Indirectly allocated:** | |
| 3,000 × 114,573/135,429 (85%) | 2,550 |
| Recoverable | 22,550 |

**Attributable to exempt supplies**

| | £ |
|---|---|
| Directly allocated | 700 |
| **Indirectly allocated:** | |
| (3,000 – 2,550) | 450 |
| Recoverable (see Workings) | 1,150 |

*Working*

Monthly average = 1,150 ÷ 3

= £383

This is < £625 per month.

Total input tax = £23,700. Relating to taxable supplies = £22,550 (above).

This is > 50%

Therefore, all of the £1,150 exempt input tax is recoverable as well as the £22,550 attributed to taxable supplies.

### Activity 7: Partially exempt trader – Multiple choice

The correct answer is:

| | ✓ |
|---|---|
| All of the input tax can be reclaimed. | |
| None of the input tax can be reclaimed. | |
| All of the input tax can be reclaimed, providing certain (de minimis) conditions are met. | ✓ |
| Some of the input tax can be reclaimed, in proportion to the different types of supply. | |

### Activity 8: Postponed accounting

The correct answer is:

| | ✓ |
|---|---|
| Australian VAT would have been applied by the seller so no UK VAT applies | |
| Imports of goods are always zero-rated | |
| The trader may charge UK VAT at 20% on the value of the imported goods as output tax on its next VAT return | ✓ |

## Test your learning

1 Business C sells goods to Business D for £384.00 plus the standard rate of VAT. Both businesses are VAT-registered.

**Required**

**(a) What amount of VAT will be charged on this transaction?**

The VAT is £ [ ]

**(b) Which business will treat the VAT as output tax and which will treat it as input tax?**

| | Output tax ✓ | Input tax ✓ |
|---|---|---|
| Business C | | |
| Business D | | |

2 **Identify which TWO of the following types of expenditure have irrecoverable input tax.**

| | ✓ |
|---|---|
| Staff party | |
| Car for sales manager | |
| Photocopier | |
| Entertaining UK clients | |

3 You have received four invoices from suppliers which show only the total VAT-inclusive price and the fact that all of the goods are standard-rated.

**Required**

**For each invoice total, determine the amount of VAT that is included.**

**Complete the following table.**

| VAT inclusive £ | VAT at 20% £ |
|---|---|
| 42.88 | |
| 96.57 | |
| 28.20 | |
| 81.07 | |

4 A UK VAT-registered business is exporting goods which are standard-rated in the UK to a US-based business.

**Required**

**Which ONE of the following statements is correct? Tick the relevant box.**

| | ✓ |
|---|---|
| The goods will be treated as standard-rated in the UK if the US-based business is VAT-registered. | |
| The goods will be treated as standard-rated in the UK, provided documentary evidence of the export is obtained within three months. | |
| The goods will be treated as zero-rated in the UK if the US-based business is VAT-registered. | |
| The goods will be treated as zero-rated in the UK, provided documentary evidence of the export is obtained within three months. | |

5 **Complete the following table.**

| Net £ | VAT rate % | VAT £ | Gross £ |
|---|---|---|---|
| | 20 | | 52.20 |
| 18.00 | 20 | | |

6 **Decide whether each of the following statements is true or false.**

| | True ✓ | False ✓ |
|---|---|---|
| A VAT-registered business can reclaim all the input tax attributed to zero-rated supplies. | | |
| A VAT-registered business can reclaim all the input tax attributed to standard-rated supplies. | | |
| A VAT-registered business can reclaim all the input tax attributed to exempt supplies. | | |
| A VAT-registered business can reclaim all the input tax attributed to both taxable and exempt supplies providing certain tests are satisfied. | | |

7 Joe, a VAT-registered trader, acquires goods from a VAT-registered supplier in another country. He uses postponed accounting to apply to his imports.

**Required**

**Tick the box that describes how Joe should deal with this import in terms of VAT.**

| | ✓ |
|---|---|
| No VAT is charged by the overseas supplier; therefore this can be ignored by Joe on his VAT return. | |
| Joe must pay output tax to HMRC at the port/airport and can reclaim input tax on the next return. | |
| Joe must charge himself 'output tax' and reclaim 'input tax' on the same return. | |

# 4 Accounting for VAT

## Learning outcomes

| | |
|---|---|
| **1.1** | **UK tax law principles relating to VAT**<br>Understand HMRC's rules about what records should be kept; electronic invoicing; how long VAT records should be retained; penalties for failure to keep VAT records |
| **2.2** | **VAT invoices**<br>Learners need to understand:<br>• the contents and form of a VAT invoice:<br>  - Simplified VAT invoices<br>  - Modified VAT invoices<br>  - E-invoicing requirements<br>  - Mixed-rated supplies<br>• how to determine the tax point of an invoice, both basic and actual, when there are: advance payments; deposits; continuous supplies; and goods on sale or return<br>• the significance of the correct tax point for: eligibility for special VAT schemes; applying the correct rate of VAT; and determining the correct VAT period<br>• the time limits for issuing VAT invoices: 14-day rules; and 30-day rules<br>• the rules relating to electronic invoicing<br>• how to invoice VAT in circumstances where the reverse charges are applicable, including under the Construction Industry Scheme |
| **2.1** | **Extracting relevant data from the accounting records**<br>Learners need to understand:<br>• relevant sources of VAT information needed by a business<br>• how to identify relevant accounting records that cover the required period of each VAT return<br>• how to identify and extract relevant revenue, expenditure and VAT figures from accounting records<br>• how to validate data and determine that the figures extracted have come from original and verified source documents |
| **2.3** | **VAT calculations**<br>Learners need to understand:<br>• how to apply bad debt relief, when this is available and what time limits apply<br>• rules for VAT when prompt payment discounts (PPD) are offered to customers<br>Learners need to be able to:<br>• calculate the impact on VAT of: PPD, bad debts |

## Assessment context

You will need to be able to explain how different VAT transactions are treated, when they are accounted for and how the VAT payable to HMRC will be affected by each transaction.

Task 6 may include a question about VAT records.

Task 2 may involve questions about VAT invoices. This task may also involve a scenario in which you need to determine the tax point of a transaction.

Task 3 could look into bad debt relief, which is discussed at the end of this chapter.

## Qualification context

This section of the notes will use your knowledge of a business's accounts. It is this information which will be used to produce the VAT return.

## Business context

The accounting system within the business will need to store information which can be extracted in order to produce the VAT return. It is therefore important to know how the VAT transactions will be accounted for.

## Chapter overview

### Accounting for VAT

#### VAT records and invoices

- Accounting records are used to record VAT transactions and verify VAT returns. Certain records must be held digitally, eg all VAT charged and paid, the time and value of sales and purchases
- VAT invoices have certain required content to be valid. Without a valid invoice, input tax cannot be reclaimed (except on certain items costing less than £25)
- Different types of VAT invoice:
  - Simplified VAT invoices – may be issued for supplies <£250
  - Modified invoice required for retail sales >£250, must show total VAT-inclusive cost
  - Electronic VAT invoices are permitted but with stringent HMRC conditions
- VAT invoices where customer will reverse charge the VAT, eg under CIS, must make clear that reverse charge applies and state the amount or rate of VAT to be charged

#### Discounts, credit and debit notes

- VAT always applies on amount net of discounts Supplier has two options re settlement discounts:
  - Invoice full amount then credit note if discount taken
  - Issue invoice with two possible VAT amounts (on price before and after discount)
- VAT invoices cannot be amended after issue
- Credit notes must be issued to correct over-charged VAT
- These reduce output tax for the supplier and input tax for the customer

#### Timing

- Tax point = usually earliest of supply (basic tax point) invoice or cash. 14 day invoice rule can override BTP
- Tax point = date used to account for VAT
- Bad debt relief can only apply where invoice more than 6 months overdue. Supplier reclaims VAT by increasing input tax

# Introduction

In this chapter we will look at the accounting records that businesses keep in order to verify their sales and purchases, and how long the records need to be kept for. We will also look at the contents and form of a VAT invoice, including e-invoicing, and simplified and modified invoices. It is important that the business raises valid invoices within the required time periods to avoid penalties, and also so that the customer can recover the input tax suffered.

Where a business offers discounts to their customers, it is important that the VAT is correctly charged. Once a VAT invoice has been issued, it cannot be amended, so any adjustments, for example returns, or changes in price need to be adjusted by credit or debit notes.

There are specific rules to determine the date that a supply is deemed to have been made for VAT purposes. These are known as the tax point rules, and are used to work out which VAT return any given supply should be included in. Sometimes, the effect of the tax point rules is that the output tax is paid over to HMRC before the payment has been received from customers. Where payment is not in fact received, the bad debt relief rules allow the business to recover the VAT back from HMRC once the conditions have been met.

# 1 Keeping records

## 1.1 VAT records

It is essential that businesses keep a record of all their transactions. Among other reasons, this is so that they are able to prove to HMRC that the level of input tax which has been reclaimed is accurate. HMRC may also want to verify that the level of output tax which has been paid has also been calculated correctly.

Generally, the information that a VAT-registered business **must** keep includes:

- Business and accounting records
- Invoices issued and received in respect of transactions within the UK, imports and exports
- Credit/debit notes issued and received
- VAT account summarising output tax and input tax

The records which are kept should relate to both the **exempt and taxable** goods and services which the business has received and supplied.

The accounting records that most businesses keep in order to verify their sales include:

- **Sales day book** – this is a record of all of the invoices sent out to credit customers, showing the net amount of the sale, the VAT and the invoice total.
- **Sales returns day book** – this is a record of all of the credit notes sent out to credit customers, or debit notes received from credit customers, for returns and alterations to invoice amounts.
- **Cash receipts book** – this records receipts from credit customers as well as other receipts for cash sales.
- Orders and delivery notes, bank statements and paying-in slips.

The accounting records that most businesses keep in order to verify their purchases include:

- **Purchases day book** – this is a record of all of the invoices received from credit suppliers.
- **Purchases returns day book** – this is a record of all of the credit notes received by the business and any debit notes issued.
- **Cash and petty cash payments book** – this is a record of all of the cash payments made by the business.

All records need to be kept for a minimum of **six years**, and HMRC is entitled to inspect these records at any time. The supporting information for the VAT returns must be easy to find.

All records may be kept digitally, and certain records **must** be kept digitally under the 'Making Tax Digital' rules. These include:

- The business name, address and VAT registration number
- The VAT on goods and services both supplied and received
- The time of supply and value of supply of all sales and purchases
- The rate of VAT applied to all sales made

While all transactions must be added to digital records, paper records such as invoices are not required to be scanned. If invoices are stored electronically, the business must be able to guarantee the authenticity and integrity of their content.

The penalty for failure to preserve VAT records, including digital records, is £500.

KEY TERM

**Cash and petty cash payments book:** A record of all cash payments made by the business.

**Cash receipts book:** A record of all cash receipts of the business.

**Purchases day book:** A record of all invoices received from credit suppliers.

**Purchases returns day book:** A record of all credit notes received from credit suppliers.

**Sales day book:** A record of all invoices sent to credit customers.

**Sales returns day book:** A record of all credit notes sent to credit customers

## 1.2 VAT invoice

VAT-registered businesses must raise a **VAT invoice** (paper or electronic) when they make a taxable supply to another VAT-registered business.

If the customer is not VAT-registered, then a VAT invoice is not mandatory, unless requested by the customer.

The invoice needs to be raised within 30 days of the supply. If an invoice is not raised, then the supplier has failed to keep proper records, and may have filed an incorrect VAT return, both of which carry potential penalties.

A taxable person can only reclaim input tax if they have a valid VAT invoice for the purchase.

An example invoice is shown below:

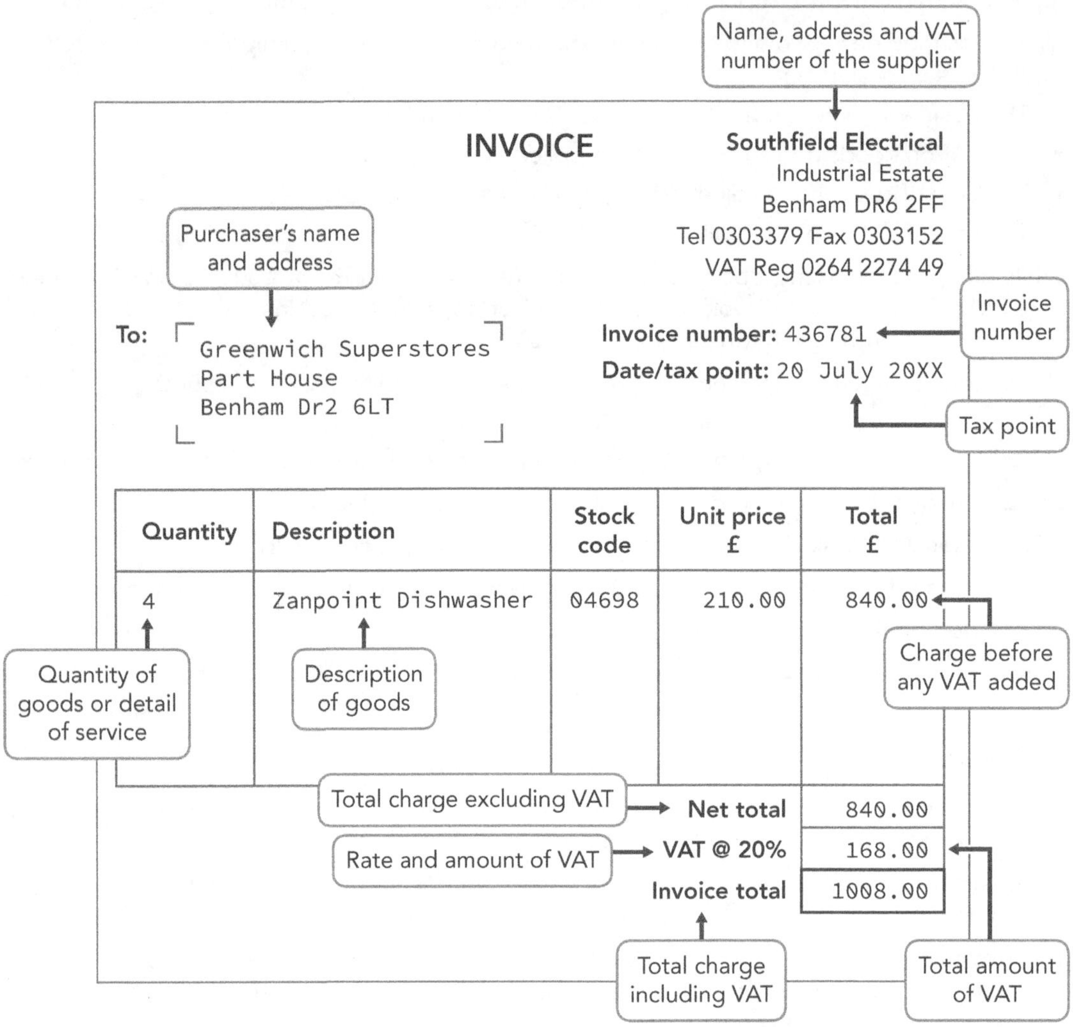


A VAT invoice must show all the information marked above. This list is included in the AAT reference material provided to you in the assessment.

Note that if supplies with different applicable VAT rates are invoiced together, the rate of VAT applying to each type of supply must be specified separately.

**E-invoicing requirements**

If invoices are to be issued electronically, HMRC require the following conditions to be met:

- The electronic invoice must contain all the required information
- The authenticity of the origin, integrity of invoice data, and legibility can all be ensured. Authenticity and integrity can be ensured by:
  - using electronic signatures,
  - electronic data interchange (EDI) with customers and suppliers, or
  - business controls which create a reliable audit trail between invoice and supply; for example, being able to link a sales invoice to the original sales order, and system controls existing to prevent that sales order from being changed.
- The customer must agree to receive invoices electronically
- The invoices must be produced in an acceptable format, for example XML or PDF
- The invoice must be securely transmitted
- The business must maintain sufficient internal controls relating to completeness, accuracy, and prevention and detection of errors, and must have a recovery plan in case of system failure

## Activity 1: Valid VAT invoice

**Using your AAT reference material, which THREE of the following items must be included on a valid "full" VAT invoice?**

| | ✓ |
|---|---|
| Customer VAT registration number | |
| Supplier VAT registration number | |
| Total VAT-exclusive amount | |
| Total VAT amount charged | |
| Total VAT-inclusive amount | |

Processing a VAT invoice will have an effect on the VAT control account, and therefore will impact on the amount of VAT payable/reclaimable by the business. Purchase invoices and purchase returns will affect input tax, and sales invoices/sales returns will affect output tax.

## Activity 2: Effect on VAT

A purchase invoice for taxable supplies has just been processed.

**Required**

**What will be the effect on VAT? Choose ONE answer.**

| | ✓ |
|---|---|
| Input tax will increase | |
| Input tax will decrease | |
| Output tax will increase | |
| Output tax will decrease | |

### Simplified and modified invoices

For **supplies invoiced at less than £250**, including VAT, a business may issue a less detailed **simplifiedinvoice**. Suppliers do not need to keep copies of these simplified VAT invoices, although the customer would still need to keep the invoice if they wanted to reclaim the input tax.

The reduced detail required on a simplified invoice is listed in the AAT reference material.

If the expenditure total is £25 or less including VAT, then no invoice is required to reclaim VAT (a simple receipt is acceptable, provided the business reclaiming the VAT understands that the supplier is VAT-registered) for the following types of expenses:

- Telephone calls or car park fees
- Purchases made through coin operated machines

If retail supplies are sold for more than £250, a **modified invoice** may be issued – this type of invoice includes everything usually contained on a full VAT invoice but also the VAT – inclusive total cost of all items included on the invoice. This information will be relevant to consumers who, of course, cannot recover input tax on their purchases.

KEY TERM

**VAT invoice:** A document that allows input tax to be claimed or output tax to be charged.

**Simplified invoice:** An invoice that can be issued if the VAT-inclusive value of goods supplied is no more than £250.

### 1.3 Invoices where reverse charges apply

If an invoice is to be issued where the customer will account for the VAT via a reverse charge, the seller will not charge VAT on the transaction, ie they will ignore the usual VAT rate applicable to those supplies. This is the case, as we saw in chapter 3, where services are supplied overseas to a VAT-registered customer, but also applies to most construction services in the UK, where the service is provided to a customer who is registered under the 'Construction Industry Scheme' (CIS). This is called a 'domestic reverse charge'.

With a domestic reverse charge, the following details must be included on the VAT invoice:

- a note to make it clear that the domestic reverse charge applies and that the customer is required to account for the VAT
- clearly state how much VAT is due under the reverse charge, or the rate of VAT if the VAT amount cannot be shown
- Legal wording to reference the reverse charge applying, for example 'reverse charge: VAT Act 1994 Section 55A applies'

### Activity 3: Reclaiming input tax

**Decide whether the following statements are true or false. Tick the relevant boxes below.**

| | True ✓ | False ✓ |
|---|---|---|
| A 'simplified' invoice can be used to reclaim input tax. | | |
| No VAT invoice is required to reclaim VAT on a car parking charge of £50 including VAT. | | |

## 2 VAT and discounts

Many businesses offer discounts to their customers.

There are two types:

(a) **Trade discounts**

(i) Given at the time of the sale/purchase, they reduce the selling price as an inducement to purchase.

(ii) Usually for regular customers or **bulk buyers**.

(b) **Settlement (prompt payment) discounts** (PPD)

If a supplier offers a settlement discount (a reduced price as an inducement to pay earlier than the normal credit terms), the VAT charged must be based on the actual consideration received. There are two ways of achieving this:

(i) Issue an invoice for the full amount, followed by a credit note if the discount is taken up.

(ii) Issue one invoice, with both possible prices and VAT amounts specified, with clear instructions to the customer regarding recoverability of their input tax.

### Activity 4: Settlement discounts

A business sells goods for £1,000 plus VAT, but allows a settlement discount of 5% for payment within ten days. The customer pays after eight days. The trader had decided to invoice for the full amount only.

**Required**

**What is the correct action for the trader?**

| | ✓ |
|---|---|
| Issue a further invoice for £50 plus VAT | |
| Issue a credit note for £50 plus VAT | |
| Take no action | |
| Issue a credit note for £50 including VAT | |

---

**Assessment focus point**

VAT is calculated on the amount after trade discounts.

Remember to look for the actual amount the customer pays if you are asked for the amount of VAT on a transaction.

## 3 Credit notes and debit notes

Once issued, a VAT invoice cannot be amended. Amending an invoice can be viewed as an act of fraud.

Instead, additional documentation needs to be created if anything about the supply needs to be amended.

If the goods have been returned by the customer or the supplier has charged too much, then the supplier may raise a credit note to offset all or part of the original invoice (including the VAT element).

The credit note will decrease output tax and will therefore reduce the amount payable to HMRC.

Alternatively, the customer could raise a debit note, which would have the same impact.

If too little was charged on the original invoice, a separate invoice should be raised for the difference.

## Activity 5: Credit note

A business issues a credit note to a customer.

**Required**

**Which of the following statements is correct for the business?**

| | ✓ |
|---|---|
| Input tax will increase. | |
| Input tax will decrease. | |
| Output tax will increase. | |
| Output tax will decrease. | |

# 4 Tax point

KEY TERM

**Tax point:** The date which determines when the VAT must be accounted for to HMRC

It is possible that an order could be received, despatched, invoiced and payment made all in different quarters.

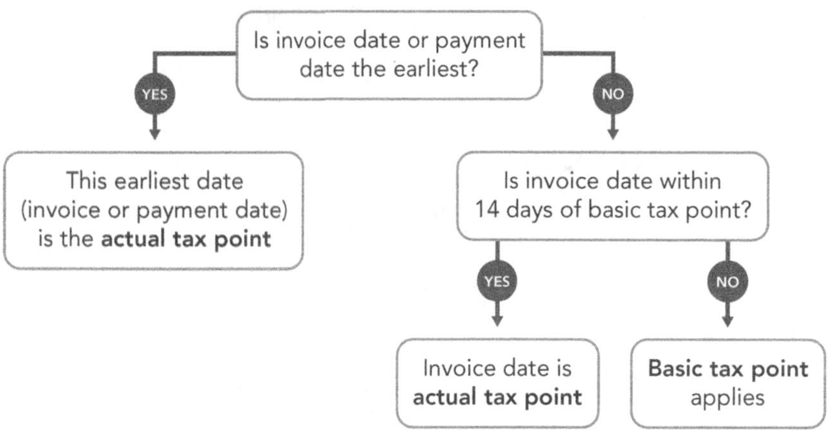


The **tax point** rules enable us to determine in which quarter to record the supply or purchase.

- The tax point is the earliest of the following events:
  - Despatch/goods made available/service completed (the **basic tax point**)
  - Invoice issued
  - Payment received

  The order date is irrelevant. Note if goods are sold on a 'sale or return' basis, the basic tax point is the earlier of the customer indicating their acceptance of the goods, or twelve months after their despatch.
- If the basic tax point is the earliest date, then check if the invoice was issued within 14 days of that date. If it was, then the invoice date overrides the basic tax point and becomes the **actual tax point**.

Businesses may contact their VAT Business Centre and obtain their agreement in order to have the 14-day rule extended.

The following decision tree should help you to identify the relevant tax point of a transaction.

First, though, you need to identify the following three dates:

- BASIC TAX POINT (date of physical supply/completion of service)
- Invoice date
- Payment date

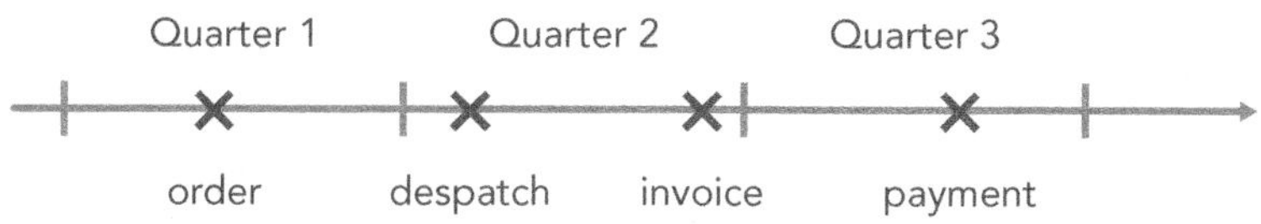


## Activity 6: Alex – Tax point

Alex raises a proforma invoice and receives a payment in advance of making a supply. The proforma invoice was dated 18 May 2025. The payment was received on 25 May 2025. The goods were supplied on 29 May 2025 and the VAT invoice was raised on 1 June 2025.

**Required**

**What is the tax point? Choose ONE answer.**

| | ✓ |
|---|---|
| 18 May 2025 | |
| 25 May 2025 | |
| 29 May 2025 | |
| 1 June 2025 | |

If a deposit is paid separately from the balance, then two tax points must be identified.

## Illustration 1: Tax point for deposits

On 1 August, a customer sent in a 15% deposit with an order. The goods were sent out to the customer on 6 August, and an invoice issued on 25 August. The customer paid the remaining 85% on 30 September.

The tax point for the deposit is determined by looking at:

- The basic tax point (delivery date) 6 August
- The invoice date 25 August
- The deposit payment date 1 August

The actual tax point is created at 1 August, as this is the earliest date.

The tax point for payment of the balance is determined by looking at:

- The basic tax point (delivery date) 6 August
- The invoice date 25 August
- The date of payment of the balance 30 September

The basic tax point is the earliest date. As the invoice date is more than 14 days after the basic tax point, the invoice date does not override it.

Tax point for the balance is 6 August (basic tax point).

## Activity 7: Bang Ltd – Tax point

On 31 May 2025, Bang Ltd ordered a new printing machine, and on 16 June 2025 paid a deposit of £6,000. The machine was despatched to Bang Ltd on 30 June 2025. On 18 July 2025, an invoice was issued to Bang Ltd, showing the full amount and the balance due of £54,000. This was paid on 23 July 2025.

**Required**

**(a) What is the tax point for the £6,000 deposit? Choose ONE answer.**

| | ✓ |
|---|---|
| 16 June 2025 | |
| 18 July 2025 | |
| 30 June 2025 | |
| 23 July 2025 | |

**(b) What is the tax point for the balance of £54,000? Choose ONE answer.**

| | ✓ |
|---|---|
| 16 June 2025 | |
| 18 July 2025 | |
| 30 June 2025 | |
| 23 July 2025 | |

The basic tax point for a service is its completion – however, if there is a continuous supply of a service for a period of over a month, for example regular bookkeeping work, the tax point is the earlier of the issue of an invoice or the payment date.

If goods are supplied on a 'sale or return' basis, the basic tax point is amended: it becomes the earlier of the goods being accepted by the customer, or 12 months after their physical delivery.

KEY TERM

**Basic tax point:** The date on which goods are despatched or services provided.

**Actual tax point:** A further date that can override the basic tax point if certain conditions are met.

## 5 VAT and bad debts

KEY TERM

> **Bad debt relief:** A reclaim of output tax when a written-off debt is more than six months overdue.

As a result of the tax point rules, output tax is often paid over to HMRC before payment has been received from customers. If a debt subsequently goes bad, traders can reclaim VAT already accounted for.

All of the following conditions must be met for VAT **bad debt relief** to be available:

(a) The debt is over six months old (measured from when payment is due), and less than four and a half years old.

(b) The debt has been written off in the trader's books.

(c) The VAT must have been paid to HMRC.

The VAT being reclaimed on the bad debt is recorded as input tax, rather than a reduction in output tax.

These conditions are listed in the AAT reference material.

### Activity 8: Bad debt relief

**What effect will claiming VAT bad debt relief have on the amount of VAT due to HMRC? Choose ONE answer.**

| | ✓ |
|---|---|
| The amount payable will increase. | |
| The amount payable will decrease. | |

## Chapter summary

- All VAT-registered persons must keep full records of the details of all trade, and details of all standard-rated, reduced-rate, zero-rated and exempt goods and services, both purchased and sold.
- These records should normally be kept for six years and must be made available to an HMRC officer if required. Certain records are required to be held digitally.
- Copies of sales invoices must be kept. The main accounting records for sales will be the sales day book, sales returns day book and the cash book.
- All invoices for purchases and expenses must be kept; otherwise the input tax cannot be reclaimed. The main accounting records for purchases and expenses are the purchases day book, the purchases returns day book and the cash book.
- A VAT-registered business making a supply to another VAT-registered business must issue a valid VAT invoice within 30 days of making the supply.
- If goods are supplied for no more than £250, including VAT, a simplified (less detailed) VAT invoice can be issued which shows only the VAT-inclusive amount and the rate of VAT; however, if the customer asks for a full VAT invoice, this must be supplied.
- The basic tax point is the date of physical supply. This basic tax point can be overridden by the actual tax point. The actual tax point can be created if an invoice is issued or a payment received before the basic tax point, or by sending out an invoice within 14 days of the basic tax point.
- If a business writes off a bad debt that is more than six months overdue and the output tax on the supply has already been paid to HMRC, this VAT can be reclaimed from HMRC as input tax.

## Activity answers

### Activity 1: Valid VAT invoice

The correct answers are:

| | ✓ |
|---|---|
| Customer VAT registration number | |
| Supplier VAT registration number | ✓ |
| Total VAT-exclusive amount | ✓ |
| Total VAT amount charged | ✓ |
| Total VAT-inclusive amount | |

### Activity 2: Effect on VAT

The correct answer is:

| | ✓ |
|---|---|
| Input tax will increase | ✓ |
| Input tax will decrease | |
| Output tax will increase | |
| Output tax will decrease | |

### Activity 3: Reclaiming input tax

The correct answers are:

| | True ✓ | False ✓ |
|---|---|---|
| A 'simplified' invoice can be used to reclaim input tax. | ✓ | |
| No VAT invoice is required to reclaim VAT on a car parking charge of £50 including VAT. | | ✓ |

A valid VAT invoice would be required for the parking charge as the VAT-inclusive cost was over £25.

### Activity 4: Settlement discounts

The correct answer is:

| | ✓ |
|---|---|
| Issue a further invoice for £50 plus VAT | |
| Issue a credit note for £50 plus VAT | ✓ |
| Take no action | |
| Issue a credit note for £50 including VAT | |

### Activity 5: Credit note

The correct answer is:

| | ✓ |
|---|---|
| Input tax will increase. | |
| Input tax will decrease. | |
| Output tax will increase. | |
| Output tax will decrease. | ✓ |

### Activity 6: Alex – Tax point

The correct answer is:

| | ✓ |
|---|---|
| 18 May 2025 | |
| 25 May 2025 | ✓ |
| 29 May 2025 | |
| 1 June 2025 | |

Ignore the proforma invoice (as this is not a VAT invoice).

The earliest date is then the payment date, which is therefore the actual tax point.

(Only the despatch date (basic tax point) is ever overridden by the invoice date.)

### Activity 7: Bang Ltd – Tax point

**(a)** The correct answer is:

| | ✓ |
|---|---|
| 16 June 2025 | ✓ |
| 18 July 2025 | |
| 30 June 2025 | |
| 23 July 2025 | |

The deposit payment is the earliest date (ignoring the order date). This is never overridden by the invoice date.

**(b)** The correct answer is:

| | ✓ |
|---|---|
| 16 June 2025 | |
| 18 July 2025 | |
| 30 June 2025 | ✓ |
| 23 July 2025 | |

The despatch date is the earliest date relating to the balancing payment. Double check if the invoice was issued within 14 days. In this case, it was not; therefore, the despatch date remains as the tax point.

### Activity 8: Bad debt relief

The correct answer is:

| | ✓ |
|---|---|
| The amount payable will increase. | |
| The amount payable will decrease. | ✓ |

## Test your learning

1 **How long does HMRC usually require relevant VAT documents to be kept? Tick the relevant box below.**

| | ✓ |
|---|---|
| 1 year | |
| 2 years | |
| 6 years | |
| 20 years | |

2 **Which TWO of the following statements about domestic reverse charge invoices are correct? Tick the relevant boxes below.**

| | ✓ |
|---|---|
| The invoice must clearly state that a domestic reverse charge applies. | |
| The invoice must include VAT at the reduced rate of 5%. | |
| The customer is unable to recover any input tax in relation to such invoices. | |
| The customer is obliged to include the correct VAT on the invoice as output tax on their own VAT return. | |

3 **In each of the following situations, state the tax point and whether this is a basic tax point or an actual tax point (B or A).**

| | Date | Basic (B)/ Actual (A) |
|---|---|---|
| An invoice is sent out to a customer for goods on 22 June 2025 and the goods are despatched on 29 June 2025. | | |
| Goods are sent out to a customer on 18 June 2025 and this is followed by an invoice on 23 June 2025. | | |
| A customer pays in full for goods on 27 June 2025 and they are then delivered to the customer on 2 July 2025. | | |

4 A VAT-registered business sends goods out to a customer on 15 May 2025. The VAT invoice is then sent later and is dated 20 May 2025. The customer paid the invoice on 20 June 2025.

**Required**

**What is the tax point for these goods?**

| | ✓ |
|---|---|
| 15 May 2025 | |
| 20 May 2025 | |
| 20 June 2025 | |

5 A VAT-registered business received an order with a 10% deposit from a customer on 2 June 2025. The goods were sent out to the customer on 11 June 2025. The VAT invoice for the full amount is dated 29 June 2025. The customer paid the remaining 90% on 31 July 2025.

**Required**

**Identify ONE or TWO tax point(s) for these goods.**

| | ✓ |
|---|---|
| 2 June 2025 | |
| 11 June 2025 | |
| 29 June 2025 | |
| 31 July 2025 | |

6 **State the conditions for the VAT on an irrecoverable (bad) debt to be reclaimed from HMRC.**

# 5 The VAT return

## Learning outcomes

| | |
|---|---|
| 1.1 | **UK tax law principles relating to VAT**<br>• Understand HMRC's rules about authorised accounting software; electronic filing and digital tax return submission, i.e. MTD |
| 1.3 | **Filing and payment of VAT returns**<br>**Understand:**<br>• the timing and frequency of: filing VAT returns under the normal scheme; payment/re-payment of VAT under the normal scheme<br>• the circumstances in which monthly accounting may be beneficial to the business<br>• the process for signing up for MTD<br>• the impact of MTD on the choice of accounting systems |
| 2.1 | **Extracting relevant data from accounting records**<br>• Understand the benefits of accounting software in identifying errors, eg incorrect VAT rate |
| 2.3 | **VAT calculations**<br>• calculate the VAT payable/repayable for a VAT period from information such as:<br>- sales and purchases invoices<br>- credit notes issued and received<br>- cash and petty cash transaction receipts<br>- deposits, advance payments and delayed payments<br>- adjustments made for:<br>◦ fuel scale charges<br>◦ bad debts<br>◦ input VAT that cannot be claimed<br>• Understand the automation of calculations through use of accounting software |

**3.2 Verify information contained within VAT returns**

**Understand:**

- what is included in all relevant boxes of the VAT return (excluding Box 2, 8 and 9)
- how imports and exports are treated on a VAT return
- the importance of reconciling the VAT return to accounting records
- how to identify reasons for any given differences between the VAT return and the VAT control account
- how statutory time limits for making payment differ depending on the payment method used
- that compatible or bridging software must be used and authorised for submitting VAT returns under MTD

**Be able to:**

- review VAT returns from accounting information
- reconcile the VAT return to accounting records

## Assessment context

Task 5 in the exam is likely to focus on preparation and verification of VAT returns. The rules surrounding Making Tax Digital could be tested in Task 6.

## Qualification context

As a qualified accounting technician, you should be able to understand the impact that certain transactions have on VAT as a whole, as well as the VAT return.

## Business context

Every registered business in the UK must generate a VAT return using the records which have been produced as part of the normal workings of the business. Almost all businesses will prepare and submit VAT returns via 'Making Tax Digital' compatible software.

## Chapter overview

**The VAT return**

**Accounting software and Making Tax Digital**

- Making Tax Digital for VAT is compulsory for most businesses. VAT returns must be filed online and certain records stored digitally
- Use of accounting and tax software improves accuracy and efficiency in preparing tax information

**VAT control account**

- Part of the business's accounting system
- Collects all the VAT transactions within the business for a certain period
- Amounts increasing VAT owed = credit entries (either increase output tax or reduce input tax)
- Amounts decreasing VAT owed = debit entries (either reduce output tax or increase input tax)

**VAT transactions**

- Irrecoverable VAT is not entered in the VAT control account
- Books of prime entry are used to post journals to the VAT account
- Bad debt relief only impacts on VAT account once relevant conditions met

**VAT periods, submission and payment**

- Quarterly (usual)
- Monthly (repayment traders may elect)
- Annually (annual accounting scheme users)
- VAT return and payment are usually due 1 month and 7 days after the end of the VAT period

# Introduction

VAT returns need to be submitted to HMRC in electronic format using authorised software. This is known as making tax digital for VAT (MTD). Accounting software automates many of the calculations, but errors can be made if items are entered incorrectly eg a standard-rated supply incorrectly marked as a reduced-rated supply. You need to be able to identify reasons for differences between the VAT return and the VAT control account.

Most businesses complete VAT returns on a quarterly basis, and the return needs to be filed at the same time as the tax paid, one month and 7 days after the end of the quarter. However, there are some exceptions to this.

VAT returns are automatically generated using MTD software, so you will not need to complete a VAT return in your exam. However, you may need to reconcile draft VAT return information to the underlying accounting records, identify why differences may have arisen, or identify which items would form part of the total of the various boxes of the VAT return.

# 1 Accounting software and Making Tax Digital

## 1.1 Making Tax digital

KEY TERM

**Making Tax Digital:** The service businesses must use to keep digital records and submit their VAT returns.

All VAT registered businesses must use the Making Tax Digital (MTD) service to keep records and submit their VAT returns. They must then continue to use the MTD service even if their turnover falls below the registration threshold.

The only exceptions to this requirement are as follows:

- If it is not reasonably practicable for the business to use digital tools, for example due to age, disability or remoteness
- If the business is subject to an insolvency procedure
- Or if the business is run by members of a religious society or order whose beliefs are not compatible with using computers

Prior to registering for Making Tax Digital, the taxpayer will need to have registered with HMRC for online services. HMRC will then issue the taxpayer with a Government Gateway user ID.

This requires the following information:

- The VAT registration number of the business
- The final month of the last VAT return submitted
- The date of registration for VAT
- The Box 5 (VAT liability) figure from the last VAT return
- The postcode of the principal place of business

Signing up for MTD is done automatically for all new VAT registered businesses via HMRC's website (unless they are exempt or have applied for an exemption), businesses should no longer have to sign themselves up: Making Tax Digital for VAT. In the event a business is not signed up, or decides to use MTD having previously had an exemption, the following information will be required:

- The business email address
- A Government Gateway user ID and password
- The business's VAT registration number and latest VAT return
- The National Insurance number of the taxpayer if they are a sole trader
- The company registration number and Unique Taxpayer Reference if it is a limited company or registered society

- The Unique Taxpayer Reference and the postcode where the business is registered for Self Assessment if it is a general partnership
- The business's Unique Taxpayer Reference, the postcode where it is registered for Self Assessment and the company's registration number if it is a limited partnership

After registration, a confirmation email is sent from HMRC.

### 1.2 Accounting and VAT software

Businesses have to be able to join up all of their records with digital links. This is done with compatible software, a list of which is available on HMRC's website.

Submission of information to HMRC under MTD must be via an Application Programming Interface (API). There are commercial software packages available that both keep digital records and file VAT returns, or alternatively "bridging software" can be used to link the business's accounting systems to the MTD platform.

Usually the information required to prepare a VAT return can be found from the business's accounting records, which are typically maintained using accounting software packages.

Adjustments to accounting information to apply specific VAT rules (for example, for recovery of output tax on bad debts, postponed accounting for imports, and irrecoverable VAT) will then need to be made by the person responsible for the VAT return, using their choice of MTD-compliant tax software. Usually bridging software is required to extract relevant data from accounting packages and make the necessary VAT adjustments.

The advantages of using accounting software (as opposed to, say, spreadsheets or paper-based systems) include:

- Reduced likelihood of errors, eg in casting
- Errors are easier to identify
- VAT amounts can be automatically computed and rounding rules automatically applied
- Compatibility for the purposes of transferring information under MTD

The choice of accounting software package may therefore be influenced by whether it has been authorised as MTD-compliant by HMRC; and whether it can store the relevant records and be used to prepare VAT returns directly or requires bridging software.

## 2 The VAT control account

KEY TERM

> **VAT (control) account:** The ledger account in which all amounts of input tax and output tax are recorded.

As businesses collect VAT on behalf of HMRC, all VAT must be accounted for separately to the business's funds. This is done by maintaining a **VAT control account**, which is a key element of the accounting system.

VAT is normally owed to HMRC and so is usually a liability to the business. Credit entries into this account will increase the amount owed to HMRC, and debit entries will reduce the amount owed.

An example of the entries found in the VAT control account is shown below.

**VAT control account**

| VAT deductible (input tax) | £ | VAT payable (output tax) | £ |
|---|---|---|---|
| VAT on purchases – from the purchases day book | 3,578.90 | VAT on sales – from the sales day book | 5,368.70 |
| VAT on purchases – from the cash payments book | 586.73 | VAT on sales – from the cash receipts book | 884.56 |
| | 4,165.63 | | 6,253.26 |

| VAT deductible (input tax) | £ | VAT payable (output tax) | £ |
|---|---|---|---|
| VAT allowable on imports accounted for under postponed accounting | 211.78 | VAT due on imports accounted for under postponed accounting | 211.78 |
| | | Net understatement of output VAT on previous returns | 287.52 |
| Bad debt relief | 33.60 | Net overclaim of input VAT from previous returns | 104.56 |
| | | Fuel scale charge | 28.15 |
| | | | |
| VAT on credit notes to customers – sales returns day book | 69.80 | VAT on credit notes from suppliers – purchases returns day book | 49.70 |
| **Total tax deductible** | **4,480.81** | **Total tax payable** | **6,934.97** |
| | | **Less total tax deductible** | **4,480.81** |
| | | **Payable to HMRC** | **2,454.16** |

These double entries will have a direct link to the **VAT return** and therefore to the overall amount payable to/repayable by HMRC in the VAT period.

In the assessment, you will need to identify the impact that certain transactions have on VAT or specifically on the VAT account. Remember, purchase invoices and purchase returns (debit notes, or credit notes received **from** suppliers) affect input tax, whereas sales invoices and sales returns (credit notes issued **to** customers) will affect output tax.

### Activity 1: Credit note – Impact on VAT

A credit note for taxable supplies is being processed.

**Required**

**What will the effect on VAT be?**

**Choose ONE answer.**

| | ✓ |
|---|---|
| Input VAT will increase. | |
| Input VAT will decrease. | |
| Output VAT will increase. | |
| Output VAT will decrease. | |

## 2.1 Impacts on the VAT account

**Irrecoverable VAT**

We know that businesses will be unable to reclaim input VAT on certain purchases and expenses. In this case, the VAT is part of the cost to the business and is therefore charged to the statement of profit or loss, or included in the cost of an asset on the statement of financial position.

For example, the double entry for buying a car for £10,000 (exclusive of VAT), where the VAT of £2,000 is irrecoverable, would be:

| | | |
|---|---|---|
| DEBIT Motor vehicles account | £12,000 | |
| CREDIT Cash account | | £12,000 |

## Activity 2: Irrecoverable VAT – Impact on accounts

You have the following extract from a manufacturing business's cash payments during the last month.

| Description | Net £ | VAT £ | Total £ |
|---|---|---|---|
| Office supplies | 200.00 | 40.00 | 240.00 |
| Purchase of company car | 19,250.00 | 3,850.00 | 23,100.00 |
| Computer | 550.00 | 110.00 | 660.00 |
| UK business entertainment | 1,000.00 | 200.00 | 1,200.00 |

**Required**

**Select either Yes or No in the right-hand box to show whether the input VAT can be reclaimed on the next VAT return.**

| Description | Yes ✓ | No ✓ |
|---|---|---|
| Office supplies | | |
| Purchase of company car | | |
| Computer | | |
| UK business entertainment | | |

## 2.2 Bad debt relief

When a business recovers the output VAT from a bad debt, this will impact the VAT account.

For example, the double entry for a standard-rated taxable supply of £5,000 (exclusive of VAT) which has become a bad debt is as follows:

To record the initial sale:

| | | | |
|---|---|---|---|
| DEBIT | Trade receivables | £6,000 | |

| CREDIT | Sales | | £5,000 |
|---|---|---|---|
| CREDIT | VAT account | | £1,000 – the business expects to collect the VAT from the customer and therefore records it as VAT owed to HMRC |

To record the bad debt:

| DEBIT | Bad debt expense | £6,000 | |
|---|---|---|---|
| CREDIT | Trade receivables | | £6,000 |

To reclaim the VAT on the bad debt (after the conditions have been met):

| DEBIT | VAT account | £1,000 – the business needs to get that VAT back, and therefore reduces the VAT owed to HMRC | |
|---|---|---|---|
| CREDIT | Bad debts expense | | £1,000 |

### 2.3 Books of prime entry

The VAT account is part of the accounting system. As such, the books of prime entry will be used to post journals to the VAT account.

### Activity 3: Books of prime entry – Impact on VAT account

Given below are some VAT figures taken from a business's books of prime entry.

**Required**

**Identify whether the entry in the VAT control account will be a debit or credit. Tick the relevant box.**

| | Debit ✓ | Credit ✓ | £ |
|---|---|---|---|
| **VAT figures** | | | |
| From the sales day book | | | 8,750.00 |
| From the sales returns day book | | | 437.50 |
| From the purchases day book | | | 5,250.00 |
| From the purchases returns day book | | | 393.75 |
| From the cash receipts book | | | 1,514.45 |
| From the cash payments book | | | 837.55 |

# 3 VAT periods, submission and payment of VAT

## 3.1 VAT period

A VAT period is the length of time covered by each VAT return.

Most businesses have three-month VAT periods and submit quarterly returns in line with their year end.

However, there are some alternatives:

(a) A business may be eligible for the annual accounting scheme (see Chapter 6) whereby only one return per year needs to be submitted.

(b) Repayment traders (those who sell wholly or primarily zero-rated goods, so will be in a VAT repayment position) can apply to complete a monthly VAT return.

## 3.2 Submission and payment of VAT

It is mandatory for most VAT-registered traders to submit their returns online and pay electronically.

In this case, their submission and payment will be due seven calendar days after the end of the month following the end of the return period.

For example, the submission and payment date for the quarter ended 31 March will be 7 May.

The exceptions to this rule are as follows:

(a) Traders who are eligible for the annual accounting scheme (see Chapter 6).

(b) Traders who are still able to submit paper returns. For them, the submission date is one month after the end of the VAT period.

(c) Traders who pay by direct debit. These businesses will receive an extra three days on top of the normal submission date to make the payment.

### Activity 4: VAT deadlines

A trader prepares quarterly VAT returns using Making Tax Digital compatible software. She always pays her VAT via direct debit.

**Required**

**Select which of the following deadlines apply to the submission of the VAT return and payment of tax in relation to the quarter ended 31 May 2025?**

| | Submission ✓ | Payment ✓ |
|---|---|---|
| 7 June 2025 | | |
| 30 June 2025 | | |
| 7 July 2025 | | |
| 10 July 2025 | | |

# 4 Clearing the VAT account

### Illustration 1: VAT account entries

In the following example, a trader has output tax due to HMRC from quarter one of £2,500. The trader pays this to clear the account before the entries for quarter two are added.

In quarter two, total output tax on sales is £3,550 and total input tax on purchases is £1,750. This results in a balance due to HMRC of £1,800.

These total amounts will be shown on the VAT return for quarter two, with the balance of £1,800 being shown as VAT payable.

**VAT account**

| Date 2025 | Reference | Debit £ | Date 2025 | Reference | Credit £ |
|---|---|---|---|---|---|
| QTR 1 | VAT paid | 2,500.00 | QTR 1 | VAT payable | 2,500.00 |
| QTR 2 | Input tax on purchases | 1,750.00 | QTR 2 | Output tax on sales | 3,550.00 |
| | Balance c/d | 1,800.00 | | | |
| | **Total** | **6,050.00** | | **Total** | **6,050.00** |
| | | | QTR 2 | VAT payable | 1,800.00 |

## Activity 5: Correction of error

A trader has VAT payable to HMRC for the quarter ended 31.03.2025 of £3,750 and VAT payable for the quarter ended 30.06.2025 of £4,200. These are the correct amounts shown on the VAT returns.

The trader pays the VAT for the quarter ended 31.03.2025, but enters it onto the wrong side of the VAT control account.

**Required**

**Identify the balance showing on the VAT control account before this error is adjusted.**

| | ✓ |
|---|---|
| £7,950 | |
| £11,700 | |

# 5 The VAT return

KEY TERM

**VAT return:** The form which must be generated and submitted to HMRC to show the amount of VAT due or to be reclaimed, usually for the quarter.

**Assessment focus point**

The VAT return (VAT 100) produced by MTD software should summarise the VAT account. This will show:

- Output VAT charged on sales
- Input VAT suffered on purchases used in the business
- Net amount payable or repayable

## 5.1 VAT return

The boxes on a VAT return which a trader must fill in are as follows:

**Box 1 VAT due in this period on sales and other outputs:**

- The total of the output VAT on sales (include credit and cash sales), plus
- The VAT due on any imports accounted for through postponed accounting or reverse charges for services
- Less the VAT on any credit notes issued
- Plus any fuel scale charges
- Plus adjustments for earlier period errors (see Chapter 8).

**Box 2** The **VAT due on any acquisitions of goods made in Northern Ireland from EU member states**. This will be £nil in the Tax Processes for Businesses exam as such transactions are not examinable.

**Box 3** The total of boxes 1 and 2.

**Box 4 VAT reclaimed in this period on purchases and other inputs, including imports:**

- The total of the input VAT on purchases and expenses (include credit and cash purchases)
- Less the VAT on any credit notes received
- Plus the VAT on any imports or reverse charges
- Plus bad debt relief
- Plus adjustments for earlier period errors (see Chapter 8).

**Box 5 Net VAT to be paid to HM Revenue & Customs or reclaimed by you:**

- Deduct box 4 (input tax) from box 3 (output tax)
- If box 3 (output tax) > box 4 (input tax), then tax is payable to HMRC
- If box 4 (input tax) > box 3 (output tax), then tax is reclaimable from HMRC

Boxes 6 and 7 deal with sales and purchases before any VAT is added. Accounting records such as purchases day books, sales day books and journals will be needed to complete these figures. Note that boxes 6 and 7 are stated in whole pounds (ie no pence are needed).

**Box 6 Total value of sales and all other outputs, excluding any VAT:**

- This is the total of all sales, **less credit notes issued**, excluding VAT. It includes:
- Standard-rated sales
- Zero-rated sales (including exports)
- Exempt sales.

**Box 7 Total value of purchases and all other inputs, excluding any VAT:**

This is the total of all purchases and other expenses, **less credit notes received**, excluding VAT. It includes:

- Standard-rated supplies (including standard-rated imports)
- Zero-rated supplies (including zero-rated imports)
- Exempt supplies

Information for boxes 1–4 can usually be extracted from the VAT account.

There are two additional boxes (8 and 9) of the VAT return. These relate to transactions between UK businesses and other EU countries prior to 31 December 2020, and to ongoing sales/purchases of goods between Northern Ireland businesses and EU member states. Such transactions are not examinable in Tax Processes for Businesses and as such the content of these boxes will not be tested.

## Assessment focus point

Because VAT returns are automatically generated using Making Tax Digital software, you will not be asked to prepare a VAT return in the Tax Processes for Businesses exam. Instead, you may be asked to reconcile draft VAT return information to the underlying accounting records, or to identify why differences between these may have arisen. You may also be tested on which items would form part of the total of the various boxes of the VAT return. The details of the contents of each box need to be learned as they are not provided in the reference materials during the assessment.

The following illustration shows the process of preparing a VAT return from accounting information in order to enhance your understanding.

## Illustration 2: Completing a VAT return

This illustration shows how a VAT return would be manually prepared from accounting records. This will highlight how differences may arise.

The relevant ledger accounts are shown below for the quarter ended 31.03.2025.

Sales and sales returns account

| Date 2025 | Reference | Debit £ | Date 2025 | Reference | Credit £ |
|---|---|---|---|---|---|
| 1.1–31.3 | Sales returns day book – UK sales | 2,374.00 | 1.1–31.3 | Sales day book – UK sales | 52,111.00 |
| | | | 1.1–31.3 | Sales day book – exports | 13,959.00 |
| 31.3 | Balance c/d | 74,041.00 | 1.1–31.3 | Cash book – UK sales | 10,345.00 |
| | **Total** | **76,415.00** | | **Total** | **76,415.00** |

Purchases and purchases returns account

| Date 2025 | Reference | Debit £ | Date 2025 | Reference | Credit £ |
|---|---|---|---|---|---|
| 1.1–31.3 | Purchases day book – UK purchases | 17,980.00 | 1.1–31.3 | Purchases returns day book – UK purchases | 1,020.00 |
| 1.1–31.3 | Purchases day book – zero-rated imports | 5,476.00 | 31.3 | Balance c/d | 22,436.00 |
| | **Total** | **23,456.00** | | **Total** | **23,456.00** |

VAT account

| Date 2025 | Reference | Debit £ | Date 2025 | Reference | Credit £ |
|---|---|---|---|---|---|
| 1.1–31.3 | Sales returns day book | 474.80 | 1.1–31.3 | Sales day book | 10,422.20 |
| 1.1–31.3 | Purchases day book | 3,596.00 | 1.1–31.3 | Cash book – UK sales | 2,069.00 |
| | | | 1.1–31.3 | Purchases returns day book – UK purchases | 204.00 |

The following journal entry has been made to reflect a bad debt that is to be recoverable this quarter.

| | Debit £ | Credit £ |
|---|---|---|
| Bad debts expense account (net amount) | 975.00 | |
| VAT account | 195.00 | |
| Sales ledger control account (gross amount) | | 1,170.00 |

In addition, you are told that a fuel scale charge of £28.83 applies for the private use of an employee's car and VAT accounted for through postponed accounting is £1,095.20.

**Required**

**Now to complete the boxes. Note that figures are shown in pounds and pence in boxes 1–5, with the figures being rounded down (if necessary) to pounds for boxes 6 and 7.**

**Solution**

*Working*

| | | £ |
|---|---|---|
| Box 1 | VAT on sales from the sales day book | 10,422.20 |

| | | £ |
|---|---|---|
| | VAT on sales from the cash book | 2,069.00 |
| | Fuel scale charge | 28.83 |
| | VAT due on imports accounted for through postponed accounting | 1,095.20 |
| | Less VAT on credit notes | (474.80) |
| | | 13,140.43 |
| Box 2 | N/A | 0.00 |
| Box 3 | Total of box 1 and box 2 | 13,140.43 |
| Box 4 | VAT on purchases from purchases day book | 3,596.00 |
| | VAT on imports accounted for through postponed accounting | 1,095.20 |
| | Bad debt relief | 195.00 |
| | Less VAT on credit notes from suppliers | (204.00) |
| | | 4,682.20 |
| Box 5 | Net VAT due box 3 minus box 4 | |
| | £13,140.43 – £4,682.20 | 8,458.23 |
| Box 6 | Standard-rated credit UK sales | 52,111.00 |
| | Less standard-rated credit notes | (2,374.00) |
| | Cash sales | 10,345.00 |
| | Exports | 13,959.00 |
| | | 74,041 |
| Box 7 | Standard-rated credit purchases | 17,980.00 |
| | Less standard-rated credit notes | (1,020.00) |
| | Imports | 5,476.00 |
| | | 22,436 |

## Activity 6: David Ltd – VAT return

**VAT exercise**

The following details have been extracted from the daybooks of David Ltd.

**Sales: UK**

| Date | | Debit<br>£ | Credit<br>£ |
|---|---|---|---|
| 31/10/25 | Sales day book | | 20,629.77 |

| Date | | Debit<br>£ | Credit<br>£ |
|---|---|---|---|
| 31/10/25 | Sales day book | | 23,673.85 |
| 31/10/25 | Sales day book | | 25,497.42 |

**Sales: exports**

| Date | | Debit<br>£ | Credit<br>£ |
|---|---|---|---|
| 31/10/25 | Sales day book | | 2,292.10 |
| 31/10/25 | Sales day book | | 2,406.72 |
| 31/10/25 | Sales day book | | 2,502.99 |

**Purchases: UK**

| Date | | Debit<br>£ | Credit<br>£ |
|---|---|---|---|
| 31/10/25 | Purchases day book | 14,231.10 | |
| 30/11/25 | Purchases day book | 15,962.63 | |
| 31/12/25 | Purchases day book | 16,436.91 | |

**VAT: output tax**

| Date | | Debit<br>£ | Credit<br>£ |
|---|---|---|---|
| 31/10/25 | Sales day book | | 4,125.95 |
| 30/11/25 | Sales day book | | 4,734.77 |
| 31/12/25 | Sales day book | | 5,099.84 |

**VAT: input tax**

| Date | | Debit<br>£ | Credit<br>£ |
|---|---|---|---|
| 31/10/25 | Purchases day book | 2,846.22 | |
| 30/11/25 | Purchases day book | 3,192.52 | |
| 31/12/25 | Purchases day book | 3,287.38 | |

- Bad debt relief on a sales invoice for £85.41 including VAT is to be claimed in this quarter.
- VAT returns are completed online quarterly.
- VAT payable or receivable is settled by electronic bank transfer.

  In addition to the above purchases, the company acquired goods with a value of £4,500 from a French supplier on 14/12/25. The VAT on this transaction is to be accounted for through postponed VAT accounting.
- Today's date is 15/01/26.

**Required**

**(a) Calculate and insert the figure to be reclaimed for bad debt relief.**

£ [ ]

**(b) Complete the following table to indicate in which box of the VAT return each item will appear.**

| | 1 ✓ | 2 ✓ | 4 ✓ | 6 ✓ | 7 ✓ |
|---|---|---|---|---|---|
| UK sales | | | | | |
| Exports | | | | | |
| UK purchases | | | | | |
| Output tax (sales day book) | | | | | |
| Input tax (purchases day book) | | | | | |
| Bad debt relief | | | | | |
| Value of French import | | | | | |

**(c) In which box(es) would the VAT on a French import appear?**

**Select all that apply**

| | ✓ |
|---|---|
| Box 1 | |
| Box 2 | |
| Box 4 | |
| Box 6 | |
| Box 7 | |

## 6 Reconciling the VAT return to accounting records

The VAT return produced by MTD-compatible software should reconcile to the VAT liability shown on the VAT control account (which of course forms part of the accounting system of the business). If it does not reconcile, the reasons will need to be identified and either the VAT return or the accounting records will usually need to be corrected.

Some of the reasons why the two may not reconcile are:

- The VAT software has been set up incorrectly; for example, it may be using an incorrect VAT rate or may have been set up to use a special scheme (for example the flat rate scheme or the cash accounting scheme – see chapter 6)
- Amendments made in the accounting systems have yet to be input into the VAT software – for example the adjustment for a prior period error, bad debt relief, or adjustments to input VAT recovery for a partially exempt business
- Amendments made in the VAT return software are not yet reflected in the accounting systems (for example the VAT on imports accounted for through postponed accounting)

### Activity 7: Reconciling the VAT return

A trader's VAT return software shows total output VAT (Box 3) of £4,800.00 and recoverable input VAT (Box 4) of £2,500.00.

The trader uses a separate accounting software package, in which the VAT control account shows output VAT of £4,800.00 and input VAT recoverable of £2,425.00.

**Required**

**Which of the following reasons would fully account for this difference?**

| | ✓ |
|---|---|
| A fuel scale charge of £75 being omitted from the accounting software | |
| The VAT software applying a rate of 20% VAT to a reduced-rated purchase with a value of £500 | |
| Failure to recognise blocked input VAT of £75 on client entertaining in the accounting software | |
| Omission from the accounting systems of VAT of £75 on imports dealt with under postponed accounting | |

## Chapter summary

- Most businesses have to use the Making Tax Digital service to keep records and submit VAT returns.
- The VAT account records the VAT payable and reclaimable by the business and is a link between the business records and the VAT return software.
- Normally every quarter the VAT return must be generated and submitted to HMRC, together with any payment, by the due date.
- The first five boxes of the VAT return can usually be reconciled to the figures in the VAT account.
- Boxes 6 and 7 must be completed from the other accounting records of the business showing sales (including exports), and purchases (including imports), all excluding VAT.
- The VAT return is generally due one month and seven days following the end of the relevant VAT return period.

# Activity answers

## Activity 1: Credit note – Impact on VAT

The correct answer is:

| | ✓ |
|---|---|
| Input VAT will increase. | |
| Input VAT will decrease. | |
| Output VAT will increase. | |
| Output VAT will decrease. | ✓ |

Output VAT will decrease.

When the original supply was made, output VAT would have been recorded. A credit note is now having the effect of reversing that sale, so the output VAT needs to be reversed down again.

## Activity 2: Irrecoverable VAT – Impact on accounts

The correct answers are:

| Description | Yes ✓ | No ✓ |
|---|---|---|
| Office supplies | ✓ | |
| Purchase of company car | | ✓ |
| Computer | ✓ | |
| UK business entertainment | | ✓ |

## Activity 3: Books of prime entry – Impact on VAT account

| | Debit ✓ | Credit ✓ | £ |
|---|---|---|---|
| **VAT figures** | | | |
| From the sales day book | | ✓ | 8,750.00 |
| From the sales returns day book | ✓ | | 437.50 |
| From the purchases day book | ✓ | | 5,250.00 |
| From the purchases returns day book | | ✓ | 393.75 |
| From the cash receipts book | | ✓ | 1,514.45 |
| From the cash payments book | ✓ | | 837.55 |

### Activity 4: VAT deadlines

The correct answers are:

| | Submission ✓ | Payment ✓ |
|---|---|---|
| 7 June 2025 | | |
| 30 June 2025 | | |
| 7 July 2025 | ✓ | |
| 10 July 2025 | | ✓ |

The submission deadline for a digital return is one month and 7 days from the end of the VAT quarter. As the trader pays by direct debit, she has an additional three days in which to pay the VAT.

### Activity 5: Correction of error

The correct answer is:

| | ✓ |
|---|---|
| £7,950 | |
| £11,700 | ✓ |

By entering the VAT paid debit of £3,750, on the credit side, the balance on the account is showing as £11,700 instead of the correct £4,200.

| Date 2025 | Reference | Debit £ | Date 2025 | Reference | Credit £ |
|---|---|---|---|---|---|
| | | | 31/3/25 | VAT payable | 3,750.00 |
| | VAT paid should be here! | VAT paid should be here! | **31/3/25** | **VAT paid** | **3,750.00** |
| | | | 30/6/25 | VAT payable | 4,200.00 |
| | Balance | 11,700.00 | | | |
| | **Total** | **11,700.00** | | **Total** | **11,700.00** |

### Activity 6: David Ltd – VAT return

**(a)** £ 14.23

£85.41 × 1/6

**Note.** This figure to be added to box 4.

**(b)** The correct answers are:

| | 1 ✓ | 2 ✓ | 4 ✓ | 6 ✓ | 7 ✓ |
|---|---|---|---|---|---|
| UK sales | | | | ✓ | |
| Exports | | | | ✓ | |

| | 1<br>✓ | 2<br>✓ | 4<br>✓ | 6<br>✓ | 7<br>✓ |
|---|---|---|---|---|---|
| UK purchases | | | | | ✓ |
| Output tax (sales day book) | ✓ | | | | |
| Input tax (purchases day book) | | | ✓ | | |
| Bad debt relief | | | ✓ | | |
| Value of French import | | | | | ✓ |

**(c)** The correct answers are:

| | ✓ |
|---|---|
| Box 1 | ✓ |
| Box 2 | |
| Box 4 | ✓ |
| Box 6 | |
| Box 7 | |

### Activity 7: Reconciling the VAT return

The correct answer is:

| | ✓ |
|---|---|
| A fuel scale charge of £75 being omitted from the accounting software | |
| The VAT software applying a rate of 20% VAT to a reduced-rated purchase with a value of £500 | ✓ |
| Failure to recognise blocked input VAT of £75 on client entertaining in the accounting software | |
| Omission from the accounting systems of VAT of £75 on imports dealt with under postponed accounting | |

If VAT return software applied a rate of 20% VAT to a reduced-rate (5%) purchase, input VAT would be overstated by (20%-5%) × £500 = £75. Hence the recoverable VAT in the VAT return software is £75 higher than the figure shown in the accounting systems (which contain the correct 5% VAT rate).

A fuel scale charge would affect output VAT not input VAT. Error 3 would result in the accounting systems showing higher (rather than lower) input VAT recovery than the VAT software, and imports using postponed accounting would be shown in both output and input VAT.

## Test your learning

1 **Decide whether the following statements are true or false. Tick the relevant boxes below.**

| | True ✓ | False ✓ |
|---|---|---|
| If input VAT is greater than output VAT on the return, VAT is payable to HMRC. | | |
| If output VAT is greater than input VAT on the return, VAT is repayable from HMRC. | | |

2 Holly completed her VAT return for the latest quarter. It correctly indicates that she owes HMRC £7,520 of VAT. However, her VAT account is showing an amount due of £12,220. VAT payable for the previous quarter was £4,700.

**Required**

**Tick which ONE of the following statements explains the difference.**

| | ✓ |
|---|---|
| The payment of £4,700 for the previous quarter has been included twice in the VAT account. | |
| The payment of £4,700 for the previous quarter has been omitted from the VAT account. | |

3 The ledger accounts shown below are those of Jamil, a VAT-registered trader for the quarter ended 31 May 2025.

**Sales and sales returns account**

| Date 2025 | Reference | Debit £ | Date 2025 | Reference | Credit £ |
|---|---|---|---|---|---|
| 1.3–31.5 | Sales returns day book – UK standard-rated sales | 398.86 | 1.3–31.5 | Sales day book – UK standard-rated sales | 10,678.25 |
| 1.3–31.5 | Sales returns day book – UK zero-rated sales | 25.59 | 1.3–31.5 | Sales day book – UK zero-rated sales | 3,581.67 |
| 31.5 | Balance c/d | 18,889.98 | 1.3–31.5 | Cash book – UK standard-rated sales | 5,054.51 |
| | **Total** | **19,314.43** | | **Total** | **19,314.43** |

**Purchases and purchases returns account**

| Date 2025 | Reference | Debit £ | Date 2025 | Reference | Credit £ |
|---|---|---|---|---|---|
| 1.3–31.5 | Purchases day book – UK standard-rated purchases | 10,850.85 | 1.3–31.5 | Purchase returns day-book – UK standard-rated purchases | 400.00 |
| 1.3–31.5 | Purchases day book – UK zero-rated purchases | 2,669.80 | | | |
| 1.3–31.5 | Cash book – UK standard-rated purchases/ expenses | 3,033.01 | 31.5 | Balance c/d | 16,153.66 |
| | **Total** | **16,553.66** | | **Total** | **16,553.66** |

**VAT account**

| Date 2025 | Reference | Debit £ | Date 2025 | Reference | Credit £ |
|---|---|---|---|---|---|
| 1.3–31.5 | Sales returns day book | 79.77 | 1.3–31.5 | Sales day book | 2,135.65 |
| 1.3–31.5 | Purchases day book | 2,090.17 | 1.3–31.5 | Cash book | 1,010.90 |
| 1.3–31.5 | Cash book | 606.60 | 1.3–31.5 | Purchases returns day-book | 80.00 |

**Journal (extract)**

| | Debit £ | Credit £ |
|---|---|---|
| Irrecoverable (bad) debts expense | 192.00 | |
| VAT account | 38.40 | |
| Receivables (debtors) (VAT inclusive at 20%) | | 230.40 |

**Required**

**Indicate which FOUR of the following figures Jamil should ensure are contained within Box 4 of his VAT return when he reconciles his accounting records to his VAT software:**

| | ✓ |
|---|---|
| Sales (net of sales returns), totalling £19,314 | |
| Purchases returns £400 | |
| VAT on sales returns £79.77 | |
| VAT on credit purchases £2,090.17 | |
| VAT on cash purchases £606.60 | |
| Irrecoverable debts expense £192.00 | |
| VAT on irrecoverable debts £38.40 | |
| VAT on purchases returns (£80.00) | |

4 **Identify which ONE of the following statements in relation to acquisition of goods from overseas under postponed accounting and how they are dealt with on the VAT return is correct.**

| | ✓ |
|---|---|
| Input tax paid at the ports is reclaimed as input tax on the VAT return. | |
| Both input tax and output tax in relation to the goods are shown on the VAT return. | |
| They are zero-rated and so no VAT features on the VAT return. | |
| They are exempt and so no VAT features on the VAT return. | |

5 **Identify which of the following statement(s) is/are correct. There may be more than one correct statement.**

| | ✓ |
|---|---|
| The fuel scale charge decreases input VAT and is shown in box 4. | |
| VAT on purchases of services from overseas increases both input VAT and output VAT and is shown in boxes 1 and 4. | |
| VAT on credit notes received from suppliers reduces input VAT and is shown in box 4. | |
| Credit notes issued to customers reduce sales and are shown in box 7. | |

6 Vincent sells standard-rated goods and services both in the UK and overseas. Sales (excluding VAT) for the quarter ended 31.3.2025 are split as follows:

- UK sales – £7,200.00
- Exports of goods – £2,705.00
- Sales of services to overseas business customers – £5,345.00
- Sales of services to overseas non-business customers – £3,200.00

**Required**

**Complete the following extract of the VAT return.**

| VAT return for quarter ended 31.03.2025 | | £ |
|---|---|---|
| VAT due in this period on **sales** and other outputs | Box 1 | |
| Total value of **sales** and all other outputs, excluding any VAT. **Include your box 8 figure. Whole pounds only** | Box 6 | |

7 Valerie is VAT-registered. She purchases standard-rated items for her business, both in the UK and overseas. She accounts for import VAT via postponed accounting. Purchases (excluding VAT) for the quarter ended 31.3.2025 are split as follows:

- UK purchases – £3,230.00
- Imports – £1,205.00
- Imports of goods from overseas VAT-registered suppliers – £8,345.00

**Required**

**Identify which boxes of the VAT return will be impacted by the above information.**

| | ✓ |
|---|---|
| Box 1 | |
| Box 4 | |
| Box 6 | |
| Box 7 | |

# 6 VAT schemes for small businesses

## Learning outcomes

1.4 **Special schemes:**

Understand:

- The thresholds and qualification criteria for the special VAT schemes:
  - annual accounting schemes
  - cash accounting schemes
  - flat rate scheme
- The timing and frequency of:
  - filing VAT returns
  - payment/re-payment of VAT
- The circumstances for voluntary and compulsory withdrawal from special schemes

## Assessment context

Tasks 1 and 8 may ask you questions in respect of the schemes. Details of VAT schemes will be provided in the reference material onscreen in the exam.

## Qualification context

As an accounting technician, you will need to have an appreciation of schemes available for small businesses. You will not need to know the schemes in great detail but will need to be able to talk about them at a basic level.

## Business context

Knowing what options are available to a business in respect of registering for VAT is important as there are schemes which can help cut the cost of administration.

## Chapter overview

### VAT schemes for small businesses

#### Standard scheme

- Default scheme
- VAT return every quarter
- 1m 7 days to submit and pay

#### Cash accounting scheme

- Frequency as for standard scheme
- Eligible if turnover <£1.35m p.a
- VAT paid and recovered on cash basis (ie ignore normal tax point rules)
- Good for traders offering long credit terms to customers
- Can combine with annual accounting

#### Annual accounting scheme

- Annual return, due within 2 months of year end
- Eligible if turnover <£1.35m p.a
- Nine interim payments of 10% of prior year liability, or 3 interim payments of 25%
- Annual liability less POAs = due with return
- Reduced admin and smoother VAT cash flows
- Can combine with other schemes

#### Flat rate scheme

- VAT liability is an industry-specific % × gross total turnover (including exempt supplies)
- Eligible if taxable turnover <£150,000 pa
- Can only recover input VAT on fixed assets costing >£2,000
- Easy VAT calculation
- Can combine with annual accounting

## Introduction

As we saw in the previous chapter, most businesses complete VAT returns on a quarterly basis, this is known as the standard scheme. There are three special schemes that you need to be aware of:

The cash accounting scheme allows businesses to account for VAT when cash is paid or received rather than using the tax point rules that we saw in chapter 4. One main advantage here is automatic bad debt relief.

The annual accounting scheme allows business to submit only one VAT return per year, instead of every quarter. However, payment is still returned to be made in instalments throughout the year based on the prior year's VAT liability.

The flat rate scheme simplifies the calculation of VAT payables to HMRC. Instead of totalling all output VAT and deducting input VAT to work out the net amount payable to HMRC, the business simply applies a percentage (generally industry-specific) to its VAT-inclusive turnover.

When registering for VAT, there are several schemes that a business may be eligible to opt for. In the exam, you will be required to be able to explain whether a business is eligible for each scheme. The four schemes on your syllabus are:

(a) The standard scheme

(b) The cash accounting scheme

(c) The annual accounting scheme

(d) The flat rate scheme

# 1 The standard scheme

This is the scheme that a business is automatically entered into when it registers for VAT. Details were covered in Chapter 5. To recap:

- VAT returns are completed on a quarterly basis.
- Repayment traders (eg, zero-rated suppliers) may opt to complete a VAT return each month.
- Payments are made one month and seven days from the end of the VAT period if the submission is electronic (with an extra three days permitted if paid by direct debit). This is reduced to one month from the end of the VAT period if it is a paper submission.

# 2 The cash accounting scheme

KEY TERM

> **Cash accounting scheme:** A method of accounting for VAT which allows VAT to be dealt with according to the date of payment or receipt of cash, rather than under the normal tax point rules.

The **cash accounting scheme** enables businesses to ignore the tax point rules and account for VAT only when it is paid and received.

## 2.1 Conditions

- The scheme can only be used when a business's VAT-exclusive taxable turnover is not expected to exceed £1,350,000 in the next 12 months.
- Businesses will only be eligible if they are not a member of the flat rate scheme (see later).
- A taxable person can join the scheme only if all returns and VAT payments are up to date (or arrangements have been made to pay outstanding VAT by instalments).
- The taxable person must also not have been convicted of a VAT offence or penalty in the previous 12 months.
- Once in the scheme, if VAT-exclusive taxable supplies exceed £1,600,000 in the previous 12 months or next 12 months (estimated), notice must be given to HMRC within 30 days and the business must exit the cash accounting scheme (they may be able to use the scheme for a further 6 months).

## 2.2 Return and payment submission dates

The due dates are the same as for the standard scheme, unless the business has also entered into the annual accounting scheme.

## 2.3 Advantages

Output VAT is not paid to HMRC until it has been collected from the customer, leading to a cash flow advantage over the standard scheme. This is especially beneficial if the business offers long credit terms to customers but pays its suppliers promptly.

Cash accounting gives automatic bad debt relief as the output VAT is only paid over to HMRC when it is received from the customer.

### Activity 1: Julie Ltd – Cash accounting scheme

Julie Ltd receives cash for most of its sales, buys most of its purchases on credit and has an estimated turnover for the next 12 months of £1,200,000.

**Required**

(a) **What is the turnover limit for ceasing to use the cash accounting scheme? Choose ONE answer.**

| | ✓ |
|---|---|
| Estimated turnover in the next 12 months is more than £1,350,000. | |
| Estimated turnover in the next 12 months is more than £1,600,000. | |

(b) **Is the business eligible to join the cash accounting scheme? Choose ONE answer.**

| | ✓ |
|---|---|
| Yes | |
| No | |

# 3 The annual accounting scheme

KEY TERM

**Annual accounting scheme:** A method of accounting for VAT which does not require quarterly returns and payments, but instead requires nine monthly direct debit payments and one annual return, accompanied by the final balancing payment.

The **annual accounting scheme** allows businesses to submit only one VAT return each year. They are still, however, required to make payments throughout the year.

## 3.1 Return and payment submission dates

The trader pays 90% of the prior year VAT liability (or of an estimate if this is the business's first year of trading) in nine equal instalments over months 4 to 12 of the VAT year. Payment is due at the end of the relevant month and must be made by direct debit.

The remaining balance is settled two months after the year end and submitted with the VAT return form.

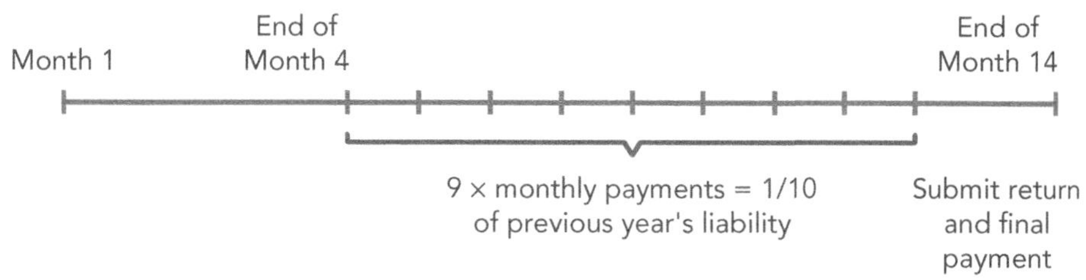


The trader may alternatively opt for three, quarterly payments of 25% of the previous year's VAT liability, due at the end of months 4, 7 and 10 in the VAT year, with the balance due with the return as for traders who make nine, monthly payments.

## 3.2 Conditions

- VAT-exclusive taxable turnover is not expected to exceed £1,350,000 in the next 12 months.
- All returns and VAT payments are up to date (or arrangements have been made to pay outstanding VAT by instalments).
- Once registered with the scheme, if VAT-exclusive taxable supplies exceed £1,600,000 at the end of the VAT accounting year, notice must be given to HMRC within 30 days and the business must leave the scheme.

## 3.3 Advantages of the annual accounting scheme

- Submitting only one VAT return reduces the administrative burden of VAT.
- The business has an extra month between the end of the VAT period and the return submission date.
- Paying a fixed amount on each instalment makes cash flow management easier.

## 3.4 Disadvantages of the annual accounting scheme

- If turnover decreases, the interim payments may be higher than they need to be.
- The business will have to wait until the end of the year when it submits its return for a refund.

### Activity 2: Thelma Ray – Annual accounting scheme

**Using the picklists below, complete the following email to a client who has had a small business for many years.**

To: Thelma Ray

From: AN Accountant

Date: 15 October

Subject: Annual Accounting Scheme

Dear Thelma Ray,

Please be advised that based on your VAT liability for last year of £90,000, and the fact that your VAT year ends on 30 September, your payments for the next VAT year will be as follows:

**Payments on Account**

[ ▼ ] will be payable at the end of each month for [ ▼ ] months. The first payment will be due in [ ▼ ].

**Balancing Payment**

The balancing payment and annual return will be due at the end of [▼] .

[▼] will be payable if you expect your liability to increase by £12,000 next year.

Kind regards

AN Accountant

**Picklist**

- 12
- 9
- January
- March
- November
- £21,000
- £9,000

---

# 4 Flat rate scheme

KEY TERM

**Flat rate scheme:** Enables businesses to calculate their VAT payment as a percentage of total VAT-inclusive turnover.

The **flat rate scheme** makes the calculation of the VAT liability simpler, by calculating the amount of VAT payable as a flat (generally industry-specific) percentage of total VAT-inclusive turnover. A 1% discount is given if the flat rate scheme is used in the first year of a trader being registered for VAT – for example, if the usual flat rate scheme percentage is 9%, the VAT liability would be 8% of total VAT-inclusive turnover for the first year of registration.

If a flat-rate trader incurs input VAT on the acquisition of larger fixed assets (those with a VAT inclusive cost over £2,000), this can be reclaimed via the VAT return. Smaller fixed asset purchases are reflected in the flat rate percentage.

If a trader has limited costs, the flat rate will be 16.5% of VAT-inclusive turnover. A limited cost trader is one whose purchases of goods are less than either:

- 2% of turnover, or
- £1,000 per year.

## 4.1 Conditions

- A business's **VAT-exclusive** taxable turnover is not expected to exceed £150,000 in the next 12 months.
- The business is not a member of the cash accounting scheme.
- If **VAT-inclusive** total supplies (including exempt supplies) exceed £230,000 in the previous 12 months (or are expected to exceed this in the following 12 months), notice must be given to HMRC within 30 days and the business must leave the scheme.

## 4.2 Return and payment submission dates

The due dates are the same as for the standard scheme, unless the business has also entered into the annual accounting scheme.

The VAT payable is calculated in a completely different way than usual, by applying a flat rate percentage to the total VAT-inclusive turnover of all supplies, so no input VAT is reclaimable (except on fixed assets as explained above).

Output VAT is charged as normal to customers.

## 4.3 Advantages of the flat rate scheme

- VAT payable is normally less than the amount payable under the standard accounting scheme.
- There will be simplified administration as VAT does not have to be accounted for on each individual sales or purchase invoice.
- Cash flow can be managed as the VAT payable is a percentage of turnover.

### Activity 3: Phyllis – Flat rate scheme

Phyllis, making only standard-rated supplies, wants to join the flat rate scheme.

The flat rate percentage applied to her business sector is 8%.

The VAT-exclusive turnover for the quarter is £40,000.

Phyllis also made purchases of £20,000, inclusive of standard rate VAT.

**Required**

(a) **If Phyllis opted for the flat rate scheme, what would be the VAT payable for the quarter?**

(b) **If Phyllis didn't opt for the flat rate scheme, what would be the VAT payable for the quarter? (To the nearest £1.)**

## Chapter summary

- If a VAT-registered business has an annual VAT-exclusive turnover of no more than £1,350,000, it may be eligible for the cash accounting scheme – under which VAT has to be accounted for to HMRC on the basis of cash payments received and made, rather than under the normal tax point rules.
- If a VAT-registered business has an annual VAT-exclusive turnover of no more than £1,350,000, it may be eligible for the annual accounting scheme – under which nine monthly (or three quarterly) direct debit payments are made, usually based on the previous year's VAT liability. The balancing payment is made when the VAT return for the year is submitted within two months of the year end.
- If a VAT-registered business has an annual VAT-exclusive turnover of no more than £150,000, it may be eligible for the flat rate scheme – under which it can simplify its VAT records by calculating its VAT payment as a percentage of total (VAT-inclusive) turnover instead of recording the input and output tax on each individual purchase and sales invoice.

# Activity answers

### Activity 1: Julie Ltd – Cash accounting scheme

(a) The correct answer is:

| | ✓ |
|---|---|
| Estimated turnover in the next 12 months is more than £1,350,000. | |
| Estimated turnover in the next 12 months is more than £1,600,000. | ✓ |

(b) The correct answer is:

| | ✓ |
|---|---|
| Yes | ✓ |
| No | |

### Activity 2: Thelma Ray – Annual accounting scheme

To: Thelma Ray

From: AN Accountant

Date: 15 October

Subject: Annual Accounting Scheme

Dear Thelma Ray,

Please be advised that based on your VAT liability for last year of £90,000, and the fact that your VAT year ends on 30 September, your payments for the next VAT year will be as follows:

**Payments on Account**

[£9,000] will be payable at the end of each month for [9] months. The first payment will be due in [January].

**Balancing Payment**

The balancing payment and annual return will be due at the end of [November] . [£21,000] will be payable if you expect your liability to increase by £12,000 next year.

Kind regards

AN Accountant

*Working*

| | £ |
|---|---|
| VAT liability for the year: £90,000 + £12,000 | 102,000 |
| Less (£90,000/10) × 9 | (81,000) |
| Balancing payment | 21,000 |

## Activity 3: Phyllis – Flat rate scheme

**(a)** VAT-inclusive turnover: £40,000 × 120% = £48,000

VAT payable: £48,000 × 8% = £3,840

**(b)**

| | £ |
|---|---|
| Output VAT: £40,000 × 20% | 8,000 |
| Input VAT: £20,000 × 20/120 | (3,333) |
| Total VAT payable | 4,667 |

## Test your learning

1 **Using the picklist below, complete the following letter concerning the annual accounting scheme to Jacob Lymstock, a client of yours who has had a small business for several years.**

AN Accountant

Number Street

London

SW11 8AB

Mr Lymstock

Alphabet Street

London

W12 6WM

Dear Mr Lymstock

ANNUAL ACCOUNTING SCHEME

I have recently been reviewing your files. I would like to make you aware of a scheme that you could use for VAT.

As the annual value of your taxable supplies, [(1) ▼] VAT, in the following 12 months is expected to be [(2) ▼] [(3) ▼] you can join the annual accounting scheme.

Under this scheme, you usually make [(4) ▼] monthly direct debit payments based on your VAT liability for the previous year. The first of these payments is due at the end of the [(5) ▼] month of the accounting period. You must then prepare a VAT return for the year and submit it with the balancing payment by [(6) ▼] after the year end.

Use of this annual accounting scheme is a great help, as it means that you only have to prepare [(7) ▼] VAT return each year.

If you wish to discuss this with me in more detail, please do not hesitate to contact me.

Yours sincerely

AN Accountant

**Picklist 1**

- Excluding
- Including

**Picklist 2**

- Greater than
- No more than

**Picklist 3**

- £1,350,000
- £1,600,000

**Picklist 4**

- 10
- 12
- 4
- 9

**Picklist 5**

- First
- Fourth
- Twelfth

**Picklist 6**

- 30 days
- One month
- Two months

**Picklist 7**

- 1
- 12
- 4

2 **Complete the following statements about the cash accounting scheme using the picklists below.**

If the annual value of taxable supplies, (1) ▼ VAT, is (2) ▼ (3) ▼ , provided that a trader has a clean record with HMRC, he may be able to apply to use the cash accounting scheme.

The scheme allows the accounting for VAT to be based on the date of (4) ▼ . This is particularly useful for a business which gives its customers a (5) ▼ period of credit while paying its suppliers promptly.

The scheme also gives automatic relief (6) ▼ , so if the customer does not pay the amount due, then the VAT need not be accounted for to HMRC.

**Picklist 1**

- Excluding
- Including

**Picklist 2**

- Greater
- No more than

**Picklist 3**

- £1,350,000

- £1,600,000

**Picklist 4**

- Invoice
- Receipt and payment of money

**Picklist 5**

- Long
- Short

**Picklist 6**

- For bad debts
- For filing VAT returns

**3** An existing trader makes standard-rated supplies and uses the flat rate scheme. The flat rate percentage that he must use is 11.5%.

For the quarter ended 31 March 20X0, the trader had total turnover of £9,500 excluding VAT. He also had VAT-exclusive purchases of £3,000.

**Required**

**(a) Which figure reflects the amount of VAT payable to HMRC? Tick the box with the correct answer.**

| | ✓ |
|---|---|
| £897.00 | |
| £1,092.50 | |
| £1,311.00 | |

**(b) In this quarter, would the trader have more or less VAT to pay to HMRC if he was not in the flat rate scheme? Tick the box with the correct answer.**

| | ✓ |
|---|---|
| More VAT is payable not using the flat rate scheme. | |
| More VAT is payable using the flat rate scheme. | |

**4** A trader has joined the annual accounting scheme for the year ended 31 December 2025.

**Required**

**Identify whether the following statement is true or false.**

| | True ✓ | False ✓ |
|---|---|---|
| The first payment due to HMRC is by 1 April 2025. | | |

**5 Would the cash accounting scheme improve the cash flow of a retail business that receives most of its sales in cash and buys most of its purchases on credit? Tick ONE of the boxes.**

| | ✓ |
|---|---|
| Yes, because they would be able to reclaim input VAT earlier. | |
| Yes, because they would pay output VAT later. | |
| No, because they would reclaim input VAT later. | |
| No, because they would pay output VAT earlier. | |

**6** A trader making standard-rated (20%) supplies has joined the flat rate scheme.

The flat rate percentage applying to his business sector is 8.5%.

His VAT-exclusive turnover for the quarter is £30,000.

He has no profit or loss expenses on which VAT is payable, but acquired two fixed assets in the quarter; the first with a VAT inclusive cost of £1,500 and the other costing £4,800 inclusive of VAT.

**Required**

**What is the VAT due to HMRC for the quarter?**

| | ✓ |
|---|---|
| £2,550 | |
| £3,060 | |
| £2,010 | |
| £2,260 | |

# 7 Payroll systems

## Learning outcomes

**4.1 Employer responsibilities of payroll**

Understand:

- that payroll is operated by businesses or individuals who employ staff
- that HMRC is the relevant tax authority for payroll
- HMRC's powers to require businesses to comply with:
  - regulations about registration
  - record keeping
  - submissions of returns
  - payment of amounts due
- HMRC's rights in respect of inspection of records and visits
- HMRC's rules about:
  - what records should be kept
  - software
  - how payroll records should be retained
  - how long payroll records should be retained
- the difference between gross pay, taxable pay and net pay
- that businesses are required to make statutory deductions from gross pay:
  - Pay As You Earn (PAYE)
  - National Insurance Contributions (NICs)
  - student loan repayments
  - pension contributions
- that businesses may be required to make non-statutory deductions from gross pay
- when businesses or individuals are required to register as an employer
- that employers are entitled to deduct statutory and other deductions from employees' pay
- the data protection principles specifically related to the personal data of employees

Be able to:

- Calculate the following:
  - Gross pay
  - Taxable pay
  - Deductions from employees' pay
  - Net pay
  - The amount due to HMRC

| | |
|---|---|
| | • Reconcile gross pay to net pay and / or taxable pay |
| 4.2 | **Operating payroll**<br>Understand:<br>• the outline content of forms produced for payroll:<br>  - payslips<br>  - P45s<br>  - P60s<br>  - P11Ds<br>• that employers must produce and distribute forms to employees within the required time period<br>• that payroll reports must be submitted to HMRC by employers in real time (RTI)<br>• the content of full payment submissions (FPS) and the employer payment summary (EPS) reports submitted under Real-Time Information (RTI)<br>• that employers must report to HMRC employee payments and employee changes within the required timescale<br>• the statutory time limits for submitting payroll returns and making payment to HMRC |
| 5.1 | **Communicating information on VAT and payroll related matters**<br>Be able to:<br>• provide appropriate information for payroll:<br>  - the completion of payroll reports |

# Assessment context

Task 7 will focus on an employer's obligations under payroll legislation.

Task 8 will require you to complete a communication to either a client or HMRC using picklists, which may involve communicating regarding payroll issues.

# Qualification context

If you are an accounting technician working for a business, you may well be involved in the operation of your company's payroll function. Therefore, a working knowledge of the relevant terminology and processes is essential for these roles.

# Business context

Payroll taxes are vitally important for a business to get right, as they affect both the business as the employer and all of their employees' tax positions.

Payroll software helps greatly with performing the detailed calculations required to arrive at the correct tax deductions and amounts due to HMRC and to the employee.

# Chapter overview

**Payroll systems**

**Payroll principles**

- Employers must register with HMRC
- Gross pay – all deductions = net pay
- Taxable pay includes cash pay less allowable employment expenses
- Payroll records are required to be kept and HMRC have the right to inspect/verify information

**Reporting PAYE information**

- Information communicated to HMRC using Real-Time Information (RTI) – FPS form on or before pay day
- EPS reconciles to FPS, contains claims, and is used if no-one is paid
- PAYE due 19th (cheque) or 22nd (electronic payment) of following tax month

**PAYE forms and payslips**

PAYE forms

- P60 – end of year summary of pay and deductions
- P11d– non-cash benefits summary
- P11D(b) – calculations of employer NIC on benefits
- P45 – particulars of employee leaving

Payslips

- Show gross pay, net pay and deductions

# Introduction

Payroll systems are used by businesses and individuals that employ staff to record salaries and wages, and HMRC has powers that require employers to register with them, keep records, submit returns and make payments.

Employers make statutory deductions from their employees pay including income tax under the Pay As You Earn (PAYE) system, employee national insurance contributions, student loan repayments and employee pension contributions. Certain other voluntary deductions may be made, for example charitable donations under the give as you earn (GAYE) scheme. The remaining take-home pay after these deductions have been made is called net pay.

In addition, employers will have other payments to make that do not come out of their employees' take-home pay, such as employer's national insurance contributions, and employer's pension contributions.

Various forms and reports are produced for payroll purposes, for example P60s, P11Ds, FPS and EPS. You need to know the contents of these forms.

# 1 Payroll principles

The entries in the accounting system that are made in respect of salaries and wages are known as **payroll transactions**. Payroll is operated by any business that employs staff.

Most businesses (and even individuals) who employ staff will be required to register as employers with HMRC, and calculate and deduct Pay As You Earn (PAYE) taxes on employees' wages. This section will look at those registration and record-keeping requirements, the terminology used in payroll and the required contents of a payslip.

## 1.1 Registration with HMRC

The objective of the PAYE system is to deduct the correct amount of income tax and national insurance contributions from employees over the year. Its scope is very wide. It applies to most cash payments, and to certain non-cash payments.

All employers, whether businesses or individuals, have a duty to deduct income tax and national insurance contributions from the pay of their employees. Setting up a PAYE system and registration with HMRC is required by anyone with at least one employee earning at least the lower earnings limit for Class 1 NIC purposes (which is currently £125 per week).

The employer must register **before** they make their first payment to an employee, but not more than two months prior to the first planned payment. Registration is done online, and HMRC will issue an employer PAYE reference number, which is required when sending payroll information to HMRC.

## 1.2 Payroll terminology

### 1.2.1 Gross pay

Gross pay is the total amount that the employer owes the employee before any deductions have been made. This will usually be their annual salary, divided by the number of pay periods in the year (for example 12 if the employer pays their employees monthly); however, it may be increased, for example with overtime payments or a cash bonus. This may also be referred to as 'gross earnings'.

### 1.2.2 Statutory deductions

**Income tax** (pay-as-you-earn or PAYE), **employees' national insurance contributions (NIC)**, **student loan repayments** and some **pension contributions** are known as statutory deductions from gross pay, because the law (statute) requires employers to make these deductions from individuals' salaries.

**Income tax**

Employees pay their income tax under the PAYE system. This means that each time an employee is paid by their employer, the income tax for that period (eg monthly) is deducted from their wages by the employer. At regular intervals the employer then pays the income tax over to HMRC on the employees' behalf.

Income tax on each employee's taxable pay is calculated using tax codes - these are provided to the employer by HMRC and summarise the tax-free pay that the employee is allowed in the tax year (a tax year runs from 6th April to 5th April each year, for example the tax year 2025/26 starts on 6 April 2025 and ends on 5 April 2026). By inputting the PAYE code into payroll software, the relevant tax rates can be applied to the employee's taxable pay to arrive at the income tax due to HMRC for the pay period.

**Employee's NIC**

Employees must also pay employees' NIC to HMRC. NIC is just another form of tax, calculated separately from income tax. An individual employee's NICs are deducted from the employee's wages and paid over to HMRC, together with the employee's income tax. NIC is calculated using relevant thresholds which change annually and are published by HMRC prior to the start of each tax year.

**Student loan repayments**

Student loan repayments are deducted from pay by employers and collected by HMRC along with PAYE. HMRC then transfers the loan repayments to the Student Loans Company, which is a government-owned organisation. When an individual earns above a certain level of income, they start to repay their student loan; the employer is required to deduct these repayments via payroll.

**Pension contributions**

Workplace pensions are also required by statute for most employers, and there is a minimum employee contribution for those employees who have not "opted out" of the workplace pension. This money is deducted from gross pay and transferred to a pension administrator to provide a pension for the employee on retirement. This would also class as a 'statutory deduction'.

### 1.2.3 Voluntary deductions

An employee may choose to have other (voluntary) deductions made from gross pay. These items can only be deducted from an employee's gross salary **if** the employer has the employee's written permission to do so.

For example, if an employee may choose to make additional pension contributions above the statutory minimum. Other voluntary deductions include trade union fees and give-as-you-earn payments to charity (GAYE).

### 1.2.4 Taxable pay

Taxable pay is the amount on which income tax is charged under PAYE. This will be calculated as:

Gross earnings minus allowable deductions

Allowable deductions are certain expenses incurred by an employee in respect of their employment duties, which HMRC allow to be deducted before PAYE is applied. They include employee pension contributions.

You will not be required to know which expenses of employment are deductible in the *Tax processes for Businesses* exam.

#### Assessment focus point

Note, employers may also apply PAYE to certain taxable benefits (ie non-cash 'perks' of employment), if these are being taxed through 'voluntary payrolling'. Such benefits are not examinable in the Tax Processes for Businesses exam.

### 1.2.5 Net pay

Once all deductions have been made, the amount paid to the employee is called net pay.

It is sometimes referred to as 'take home pay'.

KEY TERM

**Gross pay:** Total cash earnings for a pay period before any deductions.

**Taxable pay:** Amount on which income tax is due: earnings plus taxable benefits less allowable deductions.

**Net pay:** The net cash received by an employee after all deductions.

**Pay As You Earn (PAYE):** The system used for deducting tax from employees and reporting payroll information to HMRC.

### 1.2.6 Additional amounts due by the employer

**Employer's national insurance contribution (statutory)**

The employer is also required to pay an additional amount of NIC for each employee, known as the employer's NIC. This is yet another form of tax, but the difference is that it is only suffered by the employer. There is no deduction from the employee's gross pay for the employer's NIC. Employer's NIC is paid by the employer to HMRC.

**Employer's pension contribution (voluntary)**

The employer may make a voluntary contribution to the employee's pension. Again, this is in addition to the gross pay. Therefore, it increases the 'total cost' of employing individuals. However, it is not deducted from the gross pay.

## Illustration 1: Payroll transactions

Let us suppose that Ian is employed by Southfield. He earns £48,000 a year which is paid monthly. This means that each month his gross pay is (£48,000/12) = £4,000.

Remember, gross pay is the amount an employee earns before any deductions are made.

The gross amount also excludes any employer contributions made in addition to gross pay (such as employer's national insurance and pension contributions).

**Statutory deductions - amounts due to HMRC**

The payroll department of Southfield has calculated that the income tax due by Ian for this month is £590, and that his employees' NIC payment for the month should be £236.

Therefore, after statutory tax deductions have been made, so far Ian's monthly net pay is calculated as follows:

| Item | Amount<br>£ | Paid by Southfield to: |
|---|---|---|
| Gross wages | 4,000 | |
| Income tax | (590) | HM Revenue and Customs |
| NIC | (236) | HM Revenue and Customs |
| Net pay | 3,174 | Ian |

**Statutory deduction – pension contribution**

When Ian joined Southfield, he joined the workplace pension it was calculated that the minimum employee contributions were £120 per month and Southfield's minimum employer contribution was £200 per month.

Therefore, after statutory tax deductions and statutory minimum employee's pension contribution have been made, Ian's monthly net pay is calculated as follows:

| Item | Amount £ | Paid by Southfield to: |
|---|---|---|
| Gross pay | 4,000 | |
| Income tax | (590) | HM Revenue and Customs |
| Employees' NIC | (236) | HM Revenue and Customs |
| Pension contribution | (120) | Pension scheme |
| Net pay | 3,054 | Ian |

So, of the original gross wages of £4,000 per month, Ian only receives £3,054. However, the amount of income tax that he owed has been paid, as has the amount of NIC due from him, and he has also paid into his pension fund. Any voluntary deductions would further reduce this figure.

**Employer's national insurance and employer's pension contributions**

There are two further payments for Southfield to make. As we have seen, they have a statutory obligation to pay employer's national insurance contributions. This has been calculated as £537 for Ian.

And they are making a statutory minimum contribution to Ian's pension of £200. In summary:

| Type of payment | Amount £ | Paid by Southfield to: |
|---|---|---|
| Employer's NIC | 537 | HMRC |
| Employer's pension | 200 | Pension scheme |

Therefore, the total cost to Southfield of employing Ian each month is:

| Item | Amount £ |
|---|---|
| Gross pay | 4,000 |
| Employer's NIC | 537 |
| Employer's pension | 200 |
| | 4,737 |

## Activity 1: PAYE terminology

**Which of the following is the definition of 'net pay'?**

| | ✓ |
|---|---|
| Annual salary divided by the number of pay periods in the year | |
| Earnings for a pay period, less statutory deductions | |
| The total amounts payable by the employer to HMRC in a pay period | |
| Gross earnings for a pay period, less all statutory and voluntary deductions | |

## 1.3 Payroll records, software, and HMRC powers

### Payroll records

HMRC require the following payroll records to be kept:

- Amounts paid to employees and all deductions made
- All reports (FPS and EPS forms - see later) made to HMRC
- Payments made to HMRC
- Employee leave and sickness absence
- Tax code notices
- Reimbursed expenses and benefits provided to employees
- Payroll Giving Scheme documents

Records are required to be maintained for three years from the end of the relevant tax year to which they relate – so, for example, any information relating to the tax year 2025/26 is required to be kept until 5 April 2029. A penalty of £3,000 per year may apply for failure to maintain full records.

As payroll records contain personal data relating to employees, employers must ensure they comply with the General Data Protection Regulation (GDPR) when storing payroll records. This includes ensuring data is kept secure, accurate and up-to-date.

### PAYE software

Businesses will either decide to run their own payroll systems, or outsource this to a payroll provider. All payroll providers and businesses who run payroll themselves, will need to use payroll software to provide information to HMRC. Payroll software carries out the following functions:

- Recording employee details
- Calculating pay and deductions
- Reporting payroll information to HMRC
- Calculating PAYE and NIC liabilities
- Calculating statutory pay, eg statutory maternity or sick pay

Payroll software providers will update their software for any changes in tax legislation which would impact on the payroll calculations.

Free software is available from a variety of providers for any business with fewer than 10 employees. Paid-for software for larger businesses has been tested and recognised by HMRC. When choosing what software to use, employers must consider the software's functionality and suitability for the business - for example certain software does not allow different pay periods for different employees.

### HMRC powers

HMRC have the right to inspect records and to visit business premises to check that the right amount of tax is being paid. They must give the employer notice (in writing or telephone) to inform them what they want to check, and may request to visit a home or business premises or ask the taxpayer to send or bring them the required records.

# 2 Reporting PAYE information

### Reporting to HMRC – Real Time Information (RTI)

Employers must report PAYE information to HMRC under the Real Time Information (RTI) system.

Under RTI, an employer is required to submit information to HMRC electronically. This can be done by:

(a) Using commercial payroll software.

(b) Using HMRC's Basic PAYE Tools software (designed for use by an employer who has up to nine employees).

(c) Using a payroll provider (such as an accountant or payroll bureau) to do the reporting on behalf of the employer.

The employer reports payroll information electronically to HMRC, on or before any day when the employer pays someone (ie in 'real time'). This report will normally be carried out by the payroll software (or the payroll provider) at the same time that the payments are calculated and is called a Full Payment Submission (FPS). The FPS includes details of:

- The amounts paid to employees;
- Deductions made under PAYE such as income tax and national insurance contributions; and
- Details of employees who have started employment or left employment since the last FPS.

If no employees are paid in a particular tax month (for example, small companies with one shareholder-director may only pay their director a salary once or twice a year), no FPSs are required for that month. A "tax month" runs from the 6th of one month to the 5th of the next.

Instead, the employer will file an Employer Payment Summary, or EPS, form. This must be filed within 14 days of the end of the tax month (ie by the 19th).

An EPS form can also be filed in addition to the FPSs, where the employer wants to make certain claims which are not available on an FPS. These include:

- Reclaims of statutory payments, for example statutory maternity pay
- A claim for the Employment Allowance
- Reclaims of Construction Industry Scheme deductions
- Claiming NIC holidays for previous tax years
- Paying the Apprenticeship Levy, which is an additional tax on very large employers

In April 2025 the Apprenticeship Levy changes its name to the Growth and Skills Levy. The operation of the levy remains the same.

**Payment of monthly PAYE**

Under PAYE, income tax and national insurance is normally paid over to HMRC monthly, within 17 days of the end of the tax month (if paid electronically) or 14 days after the end of the tax month (if paid by cheque). Large employers (with 250 or more employees) must make electronic payments. For example, for the tax month from 6 June 2025 to 5 July 2025, payment must be made by 22 July 2025 (electronically) or 19 July 2025 (cheque).

If an employer's average monthly payments (ie the total income tax, employee's and employer's NIC) under the PAYE system are less than £1,500, the employer may choose to pay quarterly, within 17 or 14 days (depending on the method of payment) of the end of each tax quarter. Tax quarters end on 5 July, 5 October, 5 January and 5 April. Payments can continue to be made quarterly during a tax year even if the monthly average reaches or exceeds £1,500, but a new estimate must be made and a new decision taken to pay quarterly at the start of each tax year.

KEY TERM

**Full Payment Submission (FPS):** Real-time report to HMRC of pay and deductions.

**Employer Payment Summary (EPS):** Month-end report reconciling FPSs to actual cash paid to employees and HMRC.

## Activity 2: PAYE payment information

You work in the payroll department of a small company which employs 50 people, each paid monthly on the 28th of the month. After inputting each employee's pay details for the payments to be made on 28th August 2025 into your payroll software, the following information has been generated:

| | £ |
|---|---|
| Total gross pay for August | 125,000 |
| Income tax due | 22,500 |
| Employee's national insurance due | 15,300 |
| Employer's national insurance due | 17,800 |
| Employer pension contributions | 6,250 |
| Total net pay | 87,200 |

**Required**

**Complete the following internal communication to your line manager**

Dear X

I have completed the payroll for the month as requested. The total amount due to HMRC is

£ [ ] and it is due to be paid electronically by [ ].

Please review this information and inform me if any changes are required before [ ], which is the deadline for providing the Full Payment Submission form to HMRC.

Regards

AN Accountant

# 3 PAYE forms and payslips

## 3.1 Year-end procedures

At the end of each tax year, the employer must provide each employee with a form **P60**. This shows total taxable earnings for the year, tax deducted, code number, NI number and the employer's name and address. The P60 must be provided by 31 May following the end of the tax year.

Below is an image of a P60 form showing the main features:

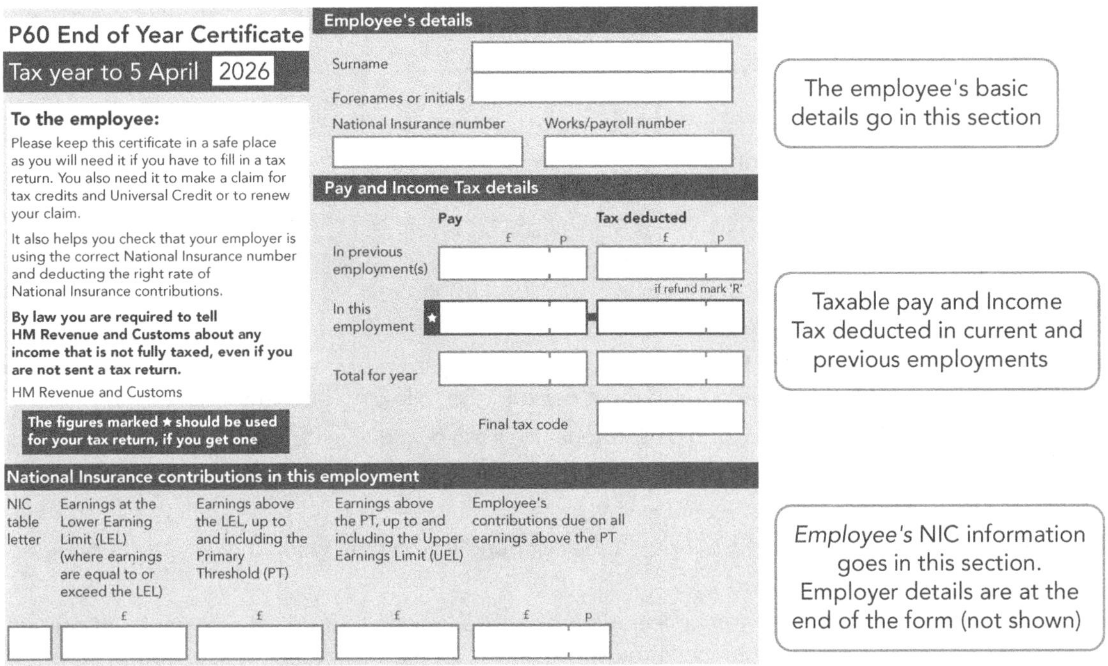
P60 End of Year Certificate

Tax year to 5 April 2026

**To the employee:**

Please keep this certificate in a safe place as you will need it if you have to fill in a tax return. You also need it to make a claim for tax credits and Universal Credit or to renew your claim.

It also helps you check that your employer is using the correct National Insurance number and deducting the right rate of National Insurance contributions.

**By law you are required to tell HM Revenue and Customs about any income that is not fully taxed, even if you are not sent a tax return.**

HM Revenue and Customs

**The figures marked ★ should be used for your tax return, if you get one**

**Employee's details**

Surname

Forenames or initials

National Insurance number | Works/payroll number

**Pay and Income Tax details**

| | Pay £ p | Tax deducted £ p |
|---|---|---|
| In previous employment(s) | | |
| In this employment | ★ | if refund mark 'R' |
| Total for year | | |
| Final tax code | | |

**National Insurance contributions in this employment**

| NIC table letter | Earnings at the Lower Earning Limit (LEL) (where earnings are equal to or exceed the LEL) £ | Earnings above the LEL, up to and including the Primary Threshold (PT) £ | Earnings above the PT, up to and including the Upper Earnings Limit (UEL) £ | Employee's contributions due on all earnings above the PT £ p |
|---|---|---|---|---|
| | | | | |



Note that net pay would not be shown on a P60; it is found by taking the 'pay in this employment' figure and deducting the 'Tax deducted' (ie income tax) and the 'employee's contributions due on all earnings above the PT' (ie employee's NI).

Following the end of each tax year, the employer must submit to HMRC by 6 July:

- **Forms P11D** – this shows any taxable benefits which have not been taxed through PAYE.
- **Forms P11D(b)** return of Class 1A NICs – this class of NIC is due from employers on all non-cash benefits.

Class 1A NIC is due by 22nd July (if paid electronically), or 19th July (otherwise) after the end of the tax year.

A copy of the form P11D must also be provided to the employee by 6 July. The details shown on the P11D include the full cash equivalent of all taxable benefits (other than those which are taxed through PAYE), so that the employee may enter the details on their self-assessment tax return.

The employer may also apply for a **PAYE settlement agreement (PSA)**, under which the employer agrees to pay the employees' income tax on certain one-off benefits. The deadline for submitting an application for a PSA is 5 July after the end of the tax year, and the associated employer NIC (called Class 1B NIC) is due on the 19th or 22nd October, depending on the payment method.

When an employee leaves, a **form P45** (particulars of Employee Leaving) must be prepared. This form shows the employee's code and details of his income and tax paid to date and is a four part form provided to the employee. One of the parts is sent to HMRC by the old employer. One of the parts is the employee's personal copy. If the employee takes up a new employment, they must give another two parts of the form P45 to the new employer. The details on the form are used by the new employer to calculate income tax due under PAYE when the payroll is next run.

## Activity 3: PAYE forms

**Match the PAYE form to its function**

| | P11D ✓ | P11D (b) ✓ | P45 ✓ | P60 ✓ | FPS ✓ | EPS ✓ |
|---|---|---|---|---|---|---|
| Tax information about an employee who is leaving their employment | | | | | | |
| Year-end summary of an employee's earnings and taxes paid | | | | | | |
| Form showing the calculation of Class IA NIC on benefits | | | | | | |
| Return sent to HMRC in a month where no employees are paid | | | | | | |

## 3.2 Payslips

HMRC require an employer to provide each employee with a paper or electronic payslip on or before their payday, and the payslip must contain the following information:

- earnings before and after any deductions (ie gross pay and net pay)
- amount of any deductions that may change each time the employee is paid, for example tax and National Insurance
- the number of hours worked, if pay varies depending on time worked (eg is paid hourly or daily)

Employers must also explain any deductions that are fixed in amount, for example repayment of a season ticket loan. They can choose to do this either on a payslip, or in a separate written statement, which must be updated every year.

Here is an example of a standard payslip highlighting the required information it contains:

| Company: | | Employee name: | |
|---|---|---|---|
| Pay period: | | Department: | |
| Payment method: | | Employee payroll no.: | |
| Payment period: | | Employee tax code: | |
| | | | |
| Bank sort code: | | Bank account no.: | |

Basic employee details to enable identification

| **Payments** | | **Deductions** | | **Year to date** | |
|---|---|---|---|---|---|
| *[Insert description of payments eg Basic salary Overtime Allowances Other]* | *[Insert amount eg hours × rate = £[insert amount]]* | *[Insert deductions eg Tax National Insurance Pension Other]* | *[Insert amount]* | Total pay to date: | *£[Insert amount]* |
| | | | | Taxable pay to date: | *£[Insert amount]* |
| | | | | **This month** | |
| | | | | Gross pay: | *£[Insert amount]* |
| | | | | Income tax: | *£[Insert amount]* |
| | | | | National insurance: | *£[Insert amount]* |
| **Total gross payments:** | *£[Insert amount]* | **Total deductions:** | *£[Insert amount]* | **Net pay:** | *£[Insert amount]* |
| | | | | | |
| | | | | **Employee NI no.:** | |

Net pay total

Gross pay total (showing hours worked if necessary)

Variable deductions, eg income tax and NIC are shown separately – other deductions may be shown as 1 figure

## Chapter summary

- All employers (whether in business or not) must register with HMRC if they will be paying an employee at least the lower earnings limit for NIC. Registration is required before the first payment is made.
- Employers take both statutory deductions (eg employment taxes and student loans) and non-statutory deductions (eg payroll giving) from gross pay. An employee's net take-home pay is their gross pay less all such deductions.
- HMRC require specific payroll records to be kept for three years after the end of the relevant tax year. Payroll software is used to calculate, store and report payroll information.
- PAYE information is reported to HMRC in real-time, ie on or before the date the employee is paid, using Full Payment Submission (FPS) forms. An Employer Payment Summary (EPS) is used in any tax month where no-one is paid, and to make various claims relating to payroll. The EPS information should reconcile to the FPS forms submitted in real-time.
- PAYE taxes (income tax, employer and employee National Insurance) for a tax month are due by the 19th or 22nd of the following tax month, depending on the payment method used.
- The following PAYE forms are used to provide payroll information to employees and to HMRC:
  - P60 - end-of year summary of pay and deductions provided to employees by 31 May.
  - P11D and P11D(b) - summary of non-cash benefits provided to employees, and the NIC thereon.
  - P45 - provided to an employee when they leave an employment.
  - Payslips - reconcile gross to net pay, showing deductions and certain key employee details.

# Activity answers

### Activity 1: PAYE terminology

The correct answer is:

| | ✓ |
|---|---|
| Annual salary divided by the number of pay periods in the year | |
| Earnings for a pay period, less statutory deductions | |
| The total amounts payable by the employer to HMRC in a pay period | |
| Gross earnings for a pay period, less all statutory and voluntary deductions | ✓ |

### Activity 2: PAYE payment information

Dear X

I have completed the payroll for the month as requested. The total amount due to HMRC is

£ **55,600** and it is due to be paid electronically by **22/09/2025** .

Please review this information and inform me if any changes are required before **28/08/2025** , which is the deadline for providing the Full Payment Submission form to HMRC.

Regards

AN Accountant

### Activity 3: PAYE forms

The correct answers are:

| | P11D ✓ | P11D (b) ✓ | P45 ✓ | P60 ✓ | FPS ✓ | EPS ✓ |
|---|---|---|---|---|---|---|
| Tax information about an employee who is leaving their employment | | | ✓ | | | |
| Year-end summary of an employee's earnings and taxes paid | | | | ✓ | | |
| Form showing the calculation of Class IA NIC on benefits | | ✓ | | | | |
| Return sent to HMRC in a month where no employees are paid | | | | | | ✓ |

# Test your learning

1 An employee earns a gross salary of £27,000 per year and is paid on a monthly basis. For the month of October, the payroll department has calculated an income tax deduction of £240.50 and NIC due of £96.16 from the employee and £274.95 from the employer.

**Required**

**What is the employee's net pay?**

£1,913.34

2 **State whether the following deductions from gross pay are statutory or voluntary deductions:**

| | Statutory deduction ✓ | Voluntary deduction ✓ |
|---|---|---|
| Student loan repayments | | |
| Income tax | | |
| Employee's NIC | | |
| Trade union fees | | |

3 **Indicate whether the following statements are true or false.**

| | True ✓ | False ✓ |
|---|---|---|
| Employer's NIC are deducted from gross pay | | |
| Employer's pension contributions are in addition to gross pay | | |

4 **Indicate which of the following payroll records HMRC require to be kept by employers.**

| | ✓ |
|---|---|
| The previous tax year's FPS forms | |
| Records of PAYE deducted from an employee who retired 12 months ago | |
| Payroll giving documents from 6 years ago | |
| Current employees' next of kin details | |
| Last year's business mileage claims made by employees | |
| Number of days' sick leave per employee in the previous tax year | |

5 **Indicate the frequency of the preparation of the following payroll forms and submissions:**

| | Picklist |
|---|---|
| FPS | ▼ |
| EPS | ▼ |
| P60 | ▼ |

| | Picklist |
|---|---|
| P45 | ▼ |
| P11D | ▼ |
| Payslip | ▼ |

**Picklist**

- Annually
- Monthly
- Monthly (if required)
- Whenever an employee is paid
- Whenever an employee leaves

6 An employee (who is paid by the hour) is given a payslip by her employer, showing the following information:

| | £ |
|---|---|
| Gross pay for the month | 550.00 |
| Total deductions | (150.00) |
| Net pay | 400.00 |

**Required**

**State two additional pieces of information that HMRC require for the information on the payslip to be valid.**

7 Alisha works for JKL plc and is about to complete her self-assessment tax return for the tax year ended 5 April 2026. She requires some information about her employment income to complete the form.

**Required**

(a) **State which form gives details of Alisha's total taxable earnings and tax deducted for the tax year ended 5 April 2026, and by which date she must receive a copy of this form from JKL plc.**

(b) **State which form gives details of the cash equivalents of Alisha's benefits received for the tax year ended 5 April 2026, and by which date she must receive a copy of this form from JKL plc.**

# 8 VAT and PAYE Administration

## Learning outcomes

| | |
|---|---|
| 1.1 | **UK tax law principles relating to VAT**<br>Understand:<br>• HMRC's rights in respect of inspection of records and visits to registered businesses |
| 1.5 | **Implications for non-compliance with VAT regulations**<br>Understand:<br>• the powers of HMRC to penalise a business that has failed to register for VAT<br>• the details of the penalty regime applicable to non-registration or late registration<br>• the consequences of late submission and non-submission of VAT returns<br>• how the penalty regime applies to late submission or non-submission of VAT returns<br>• the powers of assessment that HMRC has in respect of failure to submit VAT returns<br>• the consequences of late payment or non-payment of VAT due<br>• the details of the penalty regime applicable to late or non-payment of VAT due<br>• the consequences of failing to:<br>  - correct errors properly<br>  - report an error when required to do so<br>• the operational and legal consequences of incorrect recovery of VAT |
| 3.1 | **Make adjustments for errors or omissions in VAT returns**<br>Understand:<br>• if previous period errors or omissions can be corrected by amendments on current VAT returns<br>• the thresholds and deadlines where previous period errors or omissions must be declared, including the timescales during which corrections can be made<br>• when previous period errors or omissions must be separately reported rather than corrected on current VAT returns<br>• when to report given previous period errors or omissions that cannot be corrected on current VAT returns. Be able to process the appropriate adjustments for given previous period errors.<br>• Recognise the impact the adjustments for previous period errors will have on VAT |
| 4.2 | **Operating payroll**<br>Understand the consequences of late filing and/or payment |

| | |
|---|---|
| 5.1 | **Communicating information on VAT and payroll related matters**<br>Understand:<br>• who to report relevant information to<br>• when a query is beyond current experience or expertise and so should be referred to a line manager<br>• the significant effect on cash flows and cash budgeting of the requirements to make payments on time to HMRC<br>Be able to:<br>• communicate the appropriate time limits for submitting returns and making payments to appropriate persons<br>• communicate the effects of new legislation to the appropriate person<br>• provide appropriate information for VAT:<br>- the completion of the VAT return<br>- the discovery of current and previous period errors and omissions<br>- determining whether to correct or disclose errors and omissions<br>- penalties, surcharges and assessments<br>- the effects of a change in VAT rate or other regulatory changes<br>- the effect on VAT of a change in business operations<br>- effects of adopting special VAT schemes on payment or recovery of VAT<br>• Provide appropriate information for payroll:<br>- the completion of payroll reports<br>- penalties<br>- the effects of regulatory changes |
| 5.2 | **Legislation, regulation, guidance and codes of practice**<br>Understand:<br>• where to find information regarding changes to VAT and payroll law and practice<br>• the importance of seeking authorisation before returns are submitted<br>• the relevance of data protection, information security and confidentiality to VAT and payroll practice<br>• the importance of maintaining up to date and relevant knowledge<br>• the importance of ethical behaviour in relation to VAT and payroll<br>• the importance of updating any accounting software regarding changes to VAT and payroll legislation<br>• the importance of acting in good faith and exercising care in relation to facts or information presented on behalf of clients or employers when dealing with HMRC, according to the AAT Code of Professional Ethics. |

# Assessment context

Task 6 may ask for information in respect of errors and penalties which relate to the VAT system. There is a lot of information within the reference material which is available in the assessment.

Task 8 may require you to complete a communication to either a client or HMRC using picklists, or to consider appropriate routes of communication and review of tax information.

# Qualification context

As an accounting technician, you will need to be aware of the consequences of not completing VAT and PAYE returns accurately or on time. You will also need to know how to communicate with clients or HMRC formally, and where to look for recent changes to tax legislation.

## Business context

If tasks are not completed within a finance role, then there is a risk of the business being subject to penalties. It is important to know these consequences.

Formal communication will also be required for both internal and external communication, and it is a skill which requires practice.

# Chapter overview

## VAT and PAYE Administration

### VAT errors

- Small errors (less than error correction threshold) adjusted on next VAT return
- Error correction threshold is higher of £10,000 or 1% of turnover (max £50k)
- Larger errors or deliberate underpayment separately reported on Form VAT652

### Penalties

**VAT penalties apply to:**

- Errors (0-100% × underpaid VAT)
- Late returns/payment
- Failure to register – % of VAT due
- Record keeping – £3,000 per accounting period

**Penalties for late returns and late payment**

- Late returns
  - Penalty point per late return
  - £200 for 4 points
  - £200 for subsequent late returns
- Late payment penalty
  - See tax reference material
  - VAT due × penalty %
  - Daily penalty if > 30 days late
- Late payment interest
  - Due date until VAT paid
  - Rate × overdue VAT × n/12
  - Interest rate per tax reference material

**PAYE penalties**

- Errors – penalties as per VAT errors
- FP /EPS late – £100-£400 penalty
- Late monthly PAYE payment more than once in a tax year – penalties apply to 2nd and subsequent late payments
- Late payment of other amounts – 5-15% penalty
- Record keeping – as per VAT

### Communications

**Clients should be informed of:**

- Change in tax rates and impact on their business/customers
- Impact of registration on profitability and compliance obligations
- Taxes payable and deadlines, to avoid penalties

**Contact with HMRC:**

- Advice: check website, helpline, then contact HMRC directly
- Maintain up-to-date knowledge via websites/journals
- Control visits: HMRC must give prior notice and are entitled to question the owner, inspect records and watch the business

### Ethics

- Tax advisers must adhere to ethical principles when giving tax advice

# Introduction

Where a non-deliberate error is made on a VAT return, it can simply be corrected on the next VAT return if it is below a certain threshold, otherwise it needs to be reported to HMRC separately.

Penalties are charged by HMRC for many wrongdoings, including errors, late submission of returns, late payment, failing to register. Much of the detail that you need for this is included in your reference material in the exam, so ensure that you are familiar with this.

In your exam you will need to complete a written communication which could be to HMRC or a client. This communication may require you to determine who to report information to, or when to refer to a line manager.

# 1 VAT errors

If a business discovers any errors on VAT returns which have already been submitted, then how we treat these errors will depend on their size and the cause of the error.

## 1.1 Deliberate errors

These need to be reported to HMRC separately. This is done by contacting the HMRC VAT Error Correction Team in writing and preferably using form VAT652.

## 1.2 Non-deliberate errors

These errors need to be added together to obtain the 'net' value of errors. This is calculated as any under-declaration of VAT, less any over-declaration of VAT.

The net error is then compared to the **error correction threshold**, which is the greater of:

- £10,000
- 1% of turnover (box 6 on the return) subject to an overall limit of £50,000

If the net error is more than the **error correction 'threshold'**, then the HMRC VAT Error Correction Team will need to be contacted in the same way as for disclosing deliberate errors.

If the net error falls below this threshold, then the error can be adjusted on the next VAT return. A single adjustment is made for the net of all the errors.

The error correction threshold is in the AAT reference material provided in the exam.

KEY TERM

**Error correction threshold:** This is the threshold that dictates whether errors discovered on a previous return can be corrected on the next return or must be reported separately.

### Illustration 1: Correction of errors

A business recorded a credit note issued to a customer as showing VAT of £60.00 instead of the correct amount of £6.00. In the same VAT period, the business included a sales invoice with VAT of £300 twice in the sales day book.

The net error is:

| | £ |
|---|---|
| Output tax understated by £60.00 – £6.00 | 54.00 |
| Output tax overstated by £300.00 | (300.00) |
| Net error (overstatement of output tax) | (246.00) |

Output tax in box 1 in the next VAT return should be reduced by £246.00 to correct this error.

## Activity 1: Jim – VAT error

You discover that a sales invoice has been entered in Jim's records twice and so the VAT has been paid twice in the quarter ended 31 March 2025. The amount of VAT is £450 and you are about to prepare the VAT return for the quarter ended 30 June 2025. The box 6 figure on the last VAT return was £4,000.

**Required**

**What action should you take? Choose ONE answer.**

| | ✓ |
|---|---|
| Ignore the error as it is less than 1% of the box 6 figure for the quarter ended 31 March 2025. | |
| Add £450 to the box 1 figure for the VAT return for the quarter ended 30 June 2025. | |
| Deduct £450 from the box 1 figure for the VAT return for the quarter ended 30 June 2025. | |
| Obtain and complete form VAT652 'Notification of Errors in VAT Returns'. | |

## Activity 2: X Ltd error

X Ltd has turnover of £6.5 million. The output tax on its last VAT return was understated by £52,000.

**Required**

**Tick ONE statement below.**

| | ✓ |
|---|---|
| A correction can be made on the next VAT return as the error is less than 1% of turnover. | |
| A correction cannot be made on the next return as the error exceeds £10,000. | |
| A correction cannot be made on the next return as the error exceeds £50,000. | |

# 2 Penalties

HMRC ensures that taxable traders follow the VAT and payroll legislation by imposing fines and penalties when the trader is at fault.

## 2.1 VAT penalties

| Wrongdoing | Penalties |
|---|---|
| **Inaccurate VAT returns** | The penalty is a percentage (ranging between 0-100% - see the AAT reference material) of the potential lost revenue (ie the VAT underpaid to HMRC).<br>The penalty applies whether it was reported separately or adjusted in the following VAT return.<br>Penalty percentages are higher where the error is deliberate (rather than just careless), and higher still if the taxpayer has taken steps to conceal the error (eg falsified or destroyed invoices).<br>These penalties can be reduced to zero if the trader makes an unprompted disclosure to HMRC about the inaccuracies.<br>If the return cannot be complete on time because some information is missing, HMRC will usually permit some of the figures to be estimated and corrected in the next return. |

| Wrongdoing | Penalties |
|---|---|
| **Late VAT return** | Each time a taxpayer submits a VAT return late, this counts as a failure and each failure gets one penalty point.<br>There is no financial penalty until the taxpayer reaches the penalty point threshold (4 points if taxpayer submits quarterly returns, 2 if annually).<br>A financial penalty of £200 is charged when the taxpayer reaches the threshold, and a further £200 for each failure after that, but no further points are given.<br>Individual penalty points expire two years from the end of the month of the failure. For example, a return for the quarter ended 31 March 2026 would be due on 7 May 2026, if it was submitted late a point would be given, but would expire on 31 May 2028.<br>However, once at the threshold, the points no longer expire after two years. For their points to be reset to zero, the taxpayer has to:<br>1. complete a period of compliance where there are no further failures AND<br>2. have submitted all VAT returns due in the last 24 months<br>The period of compliance is 12 months for quarterly returns (24 months for annual submissions)<br>Penalties and penalty points apply to nil and repayment returns as well as returns that show a liability. |
| **Late VAT payment** | **Late payment penalty**<br>If the VAT is paid late to HMRC, then no penalty is payable as long as the liability is settled within 15 days of the due date or a time to pay arrangements has been agreed with HMRC.<br>If the VAT is outstanding after 15 days a penalty is charged. This will be 3% of the amount outstanding at the end of day 15.<br>A further 3% is charged at the end of day 30 if the VAT is still outstanding.<br>10% per annum is charged on unpaid VAT from day 31 onwards, calculated on a daily basis.<br>**Interest charged**<br>Interest is calculated at the Bank of England base rate plus 4%. The base rate is given in the assessment. |
| **Failure to register for VAT** | Traders need to ensure that they are completing the historic and future tests on a regular basis.<br>Once they have identified the need to register, they must do so within 30 days of the test date.<br>The penalty will be based on a percentage of the VAT due from the date registration was supposed to occur. |
| **Failure to keep and retain records** | All records must be kept for at least six years, unless HMRC gives written permission for a shorter period. Where records have not been retained for this period, there is a penalty of £500. |

## Activity 3: Late VAT returns

The VAT-registered business you work for, has submitted its recent VAT returns and paid its tax as follows:

| Quarter ended | Return submitted |
|---|---|
| 31 March 2025 | 15 May 2025 |
| 30 June 2025 | 31 August 2025 |
| 30 September 2025 | 5 November 2025 |
| 31 December 2025 | 21 February 2026 |
| 31 March 2026 | 7 May 2026 |
| 30 June 2026 | 7 August 2026 |
| 30 September 2026 | 7 November 2026 |
| 31 December 2026 | 7 February 2027 |

Prior to 31 March 2025, all VAT returns had been submitted (and VAT liabilities paid) on time.

**Required**

**On 8 February 2027, how many penalty points does the business have?**

| | ✓ |
|---|---|
| 0 | |
| 2 | |
| 3 | |
| 4 | |

## Activity 4: Late payment of VAT

Haycock Ltd paid its VAT liabilities late for the quarters ended 31 March 2025, 30 June 2025 and 30 September 2025.

| Quarter end | VAT liability | Paid |
|---|---|---|
| 31 March 2025 | £22,000 | 7 days late |
| 30 June 2025 | £32,000 | 19 days late |

| Quarter end | VAT liability | Paid |
|---|---|---|
| 30 September 2025 | £15,000 | 46 days late |

**Required**

**What penalties are payable in relation to each quarter?**

Answer to the nearest pound.

The penalty for late payment in respect of the quarter ended 31 March 2025 is £ [ ]

The penalty for late payment in respect of the quarter ended 30 June 2025 is £ [ ]

The penalty for late payment in respect of the quarter ended 30 September 2025 is £ [ ]

---

## 2.2 PAYE penalties

| Wrongdoing | Penalties |
|---|---|
| **Careless and deliberate errors and inaccurate payroll filings** | The penalty system for errors is the same as for VAT – a penalty is charged as a percentage of underpaid payroll taxes and will depend on whether the error is careless or deliberate, and whether prompted or unprompted disclosure has been made to HMRC. |
| **Late submission of payroll filings** | If an FPS is late, insufficient FPSs are filed or an EPS is not filed, a penalty of between £100 and £400 is imposed per month, depending on the number of employees a business has (see reference material).<br>These penalties may be waived under certain circumstances, for example:<br>• All payroll payments have been made to HMRC within 3 days of the employees being paid<br>• A new employer submits their FPS within 30 days of first paying an employee<br>• It is the first late filing in a tax year.<br>See Illustration 2 below. |
| **Late payroll payment** | One late payment in a tax year does not trigger a penalty. Any more than one late payment (known as a 'default') will trigger a penalty of between 1% and 4% of the late paid tax. Your reference material shows the percentage to be applied to the tax due.<br>If any payments (including the first late payment in the year, on which 'normal' penalties do not apply) are more than 6 months late, an extra 5% penalty is due, and a further 5% penalty applies to payments more than 12 months late.<br>See Illustration 2 below. |

| Wrongdoing | Penalties |
|---|---|
| **Late payment of other amounts due to HMRC** | Other payroll taxes due (for example, Class 1A NIC on benefits) suffer penalties of:<br>5% if over 30 days late<br>An additional 5% if over 6 months late<br>An additional 5% if over 12 months late |
| **Failure to keep and retain records** | All PAYE records must be kept for at least three years, unless HMRC gives written permission for a shorter period. Where records have not been retained for this period, there is a maximum penalty of £3,000 per accounting period. |

### Illustration 2: PAYE penalties

Jonathan is a sole trader employing 15 people and has a consistent payroll tax liability of £4,000 per month. He pays this late on six occasions during the tax year 2025/26. All of the late payments were made within 14 days of their due dates except for the final late payment which was 8 months overdue.

Each time Jonathan paid his PAYE late, he also submitted the FPS late.

The penalties imposed on Jonathan in respect of the tax year 2025/26 are as follows:

*Late filing of FPS*

Jonathan has 15 employees so the penalty is £200 per month, excluding the first late filing: £200 × 5 = £1,000.

*Late payment of PAYE:*

First late payment has no penalty imposed.

Remaining late payments (defaults):

Defaults 1-3: £4,000 × 3 × 1% = £120

Defaults 4-5: £4,000 × 2 × 2% = £160

Additional penalty for payment more than 6 months overdue: 5% × £4,000 = £200.

## 2.3 Assessments

The majority of penalties are based on the VAT or payroll taxes which are due to HMRC.

If no VAT return or FPS is submitted, HMRC can raise an assessment based on what it believes is owed.

The penalty is then calculated on this amount.

The trader then has 30 days to notify HMRC if the amount owed is actually greater. If this is not done, then they may be liable to another penalty.

## 2.4 Fraudulent evasion

Tax evasion is a criminal offence and this will result in fines and/or (in extreme cases) imprisonment.

**Tax evasion:**

- Misleading HMRC by suppressing information or deliberately providing false information
- Illegal

**Tax avoidance:**

- Using the legislation to minimise your tax burden
- Legal

KEY TERM

**Tax evasion:** Falsely reclaiming input tax/understating output tax or payroll taxes, obtaining bad debt relief or obtaining a repayment to which the business is not entitled.

# 3 Communications

In the exam, you will need to complete a written communication to HMRC or to a client.

This communication could be on anything you have seen in your VAT and payroll studies so far, ie contacting a client to discuss what VAT is payable to HMRC and when, or it could be in respect of the following.

## 3.1 Contact with HMRC

### 3.1.1 Seeking advice on VAT legislation

HMRC will expect taxpayers to go through the following process:

(a) Check the **HMRC website** – this can usually resolve most queries.

(b) Telephone the VAT helpline – with VAT registration number and postcode.

(c) Write to HMRC – preferably by email.

Any communication must always be carried out in a polite and professional manner. You should always keep a record of any communication with HMRC.

KEY TERM

**HMRC website:** The first place a taxpayer must check to try and resolve any VAT queries.

### 3.1.2 Control visits

HMRC officers may visit a VAT-registered business to determine whether their VAT records are correct and up to date. They are entitled to do the following activities:

(a) Question the business owner, or the person responsible for keeping the VAT records.

(b) Examine business records.

(c) Check the VAT return is accurate.

(d) Watch business activity.

The officer will need to contact the business owner in writing at least seven days before the visit.

## 3.2 Maintaining up-to-date tax knowledge

Tax advisers need to keep up to date with the VAT and payroll legislation to ensure that they keep their clients compliant and avoid penalties.

Legislation changes can be found:

(a) On the HMRC and government websites.

(b) In direct communications with HMRC.

(c) In technical circulars within accountancy firms.

(d) In specialist journals.

Changes in practice may be identified by:

(a) Attending continual professional development (CPD) briefings.

(b) Reading relevant journals.

(c) Meeting other professionals.

## 3.3 Changes in tax legislation

Changes to the tax legislation can have an impact on a number of things.

### 3.3.1 Accounting systems

If the VAT rate changes, in general or just for a specific product, then IT systems will need to be updated for the new rates. Income tax and national insurance thresholds and allowances generally change once per year so payroll software will require updating for this.

Users of taxation software should ensure they are aware of required updates to the software, for example by maintaining an awareness of changes in VAT or payroll legislation (see section 3.2) or by following notifications from the software provider.

### 3.3.2 Change in VAT rate - impact on customers

If the business's customers are all VAT-registered and making taxable supplies, then the change in VAT will not impact them as they will be able to recover the input tax they have suffered. However, if they are not VAT-registered or partially exempt, then an increase to the VAT rate will increase the cost of that product for the customer.

The supplier will have to consider whether to raise their prices (thus passing the VAT increase on to their customers) or to keep prices the same, and therefore retain less of the sales revenue. For example, an increase in the VAT rate from 20% to 22% on a net sale of £100 could be dealt with as follows:

Option 1: raise prices

The selling price would go from £120 (£100 × 120%) to £122 (£100 × 122%)

Option 2: keep prices the same

The previous selling price of £120 would now represent 122% of the net price. Therefore the trader would owe £21.64 (£120 × 22/122) to HMRC and would retain the remaining £98.36. The customer would not bear any of the additional VAT cost but the trader's net profit would fall.

### 3.3.3 Non-VAT-registered businesses

If the VAT registration threshold changes, then this could mean that some businesses may need to register earlier or later than expected.

## Activity 5: Ian Morris – Client communication

You are a trainee accounting technician working for a sole trader, Mr Shelton. Mr Shelton has just received a letter from a client, Ian Morris (a trader making only standard-rated supplies to non-registered clients), asking about the impact of a recent change in the standard rate of VAT on his clients. The rate changed from 20% to 25%. He is undecided about whether to change his prices.

**Required**

**You are required to complete the following letter to Ian Morris discussing the options open to him.**

To: Ian Morris

From: Mr Shelton

Date: 30 December

Subject: Change of VAT rate

Dear Ian Morris,

Further to your recent email, I have set out below the options open to you in relation to the standard rate of VAT.

Until recently, you have been charging VAT at a rate of (1) | (1) ▼ | . Therefore, a VAT-exclusive sale with a value of £1,000 has cost your non-registered clients (2) £ | (2) ▼ |

.

The two options open to you are as follows:

- Keep the same VAT-exclusive value of £1,000.

The benefit of this option is that you have the same amount of VAT-exclusive sales value per item sold. However, this will now make the VAT-inclusive cost to your customers higher at (3) £ | (3) ▼ | . This may make your prices less competitive (if your competitors do not do the same) and may result in a loss of some customers.

- Keep the same VAT-inclusive value of (4) £ | (4) ▼ | .

Under this alternative option, you will remain competitive to your customers. However, your VAT-exclusive sales value per item sold will be reduced to (5) £ | (5) ▼ | .

There is no obvious correct option to choose; it will depend primarily on the strength of your competitors.

If you wish to discuss this with me in more detail, please do not hesitate to contact me.

Yours sincerely,

Mr Shelton

**Picklist 1**

- 0%
- 20%
- 25%

**Picklist 2**

- 1,000
- 1,200
- 1,500

**Picklist 3**

- 1,000
- 1,200
- 1,250

**Picklist 4**

- 1,000
- 1,200
- 1,250

**Picklist 5**

- 1,000
- 800
- 960

## 3.4 Client communication

The following factors should be considered when communicating with clients:

- Communication should be timely - payment of tax may have a significant effect on a business's cash flows and therefore prompt information, especially of unexpected liabilities, is essential.
- Advice should be accurate - technical issues over which a tax adviser is uncertain should be referred to a line manager before being communicated to a client.
- When acting as a tax agent, the client's authorisation is required to submit information (returns or responses to enquiries) to HMRC. Ultimately the client is responsible for the information being provided and should be aware of this.
- When information is communicated, security measures are necessary in order to ensure compliance with the General Data Protection Regulation (GDPR) and the fundamental ethical principle of confidentiality (see below).

# 4 Ethics

## 4.1 Fundamental principles

Working in tax requires adherence to the following five fundamental ethical principles:

- **Integrity.** Being straightforward and honest in all business relationships.
- **Objectivity.** Refusing to allow bias, conflicts of interest or undue influence to override professional judgements.
- **Professional competence and due care.** A professional accountant has an obligation to keep their knowledge and skills at a level that enables clients to receive a competent professional service, and to act diligently when providing those services.
- **Confidentiality.** Respecting the confidentiality of client information and keeping it confidential unless there is a legal or professional obligation to disclose it.
- **Professional behaviour.** Compliance with relevant laws and regulations to avoid discrediting the profession.

### Activity 6: Fundamental principles

You work in the tax department of a large company. You have prepared the VAT return for the quarter and submitted it to your Finance Director for her review. On reviewing your draft return, she has asked you to amend it in order reclaim all the VAT on a party, at which several clients were in attendance. She mentioned at the end of the conversation that your annual performance appraisal was due.

**Required**

**Which fundamental principles could be breached if you agreed to her request?**

**Tick THREE boxes.**

| | ✓ |
|---|---|
| Integrity | |
| Objectivity | |
| Professional competence and due care | |
| Confidentiality | |
| Professional behaviour | |

## Chapter summary

- If a net error smaller than the error correction reporting threshold is discovered from a previous tax period, it can be corrected in the next VAT return.
- If a net error exceeding the error correction reporting threshold is discovered from a previous tax period, it cannot be adjusted in the next VAT return. Instead, a voluntary disclosure should be made and the HMRC VAT Error Correction Team informed. A penalty might be imposed, depending on the behaviour of the business.
- If a VAT return is late, the taxpayer gets a penalty point and a further penalty point for each subsequent late filing. Once the number of points reach the threshold a penalty of £200 is charged for each late filing. The points expire after two years but if the threshold has been reached the points remain until the taxpayer has completed a period of compliance and all VAT returns for the last two years have been submitted.
- If a payment of VAT is late, there is no penalty so long as it is paid within 15 days of the due date. If it is outstanding for longer than 15 days then a penalty of 3% of the outstanding balance at the end of day 15 is charged. A further penalty of 3% is charged based on the outstanding balance at the end of day 30 and then 10%, charged on a daily basis is applied if the VAT remains unpaid beyond day 30.
- Similarly, late filing or payment of PAYE taxes can result in penalties being charged.
- A number of other penalties pertain to both VAT and payroll taxes, including for failure to register and failure to keep records.
- Tax evasion is a criminal offence and may give rise to fines and/or imprisonment.
- VAT and payroll taxes can be substantial payments for a business. Therefore steps must be taken to ensure both the return and any payment can be made by the due dates.
- Changes in tax legislation can have a significant impact on accounting and tax software systems.
- Staff and customers need to be informed of a change to the VAT rate.
- HMRC expect taxpayers to try and resolve any queries by checking their website before telephoning or writing to them. However, sometimes written confirmation about an issue should be insisted upon.
- HMRC officers may, from time to time, visit a VAT-registered business to check on VAT records, or the payroll records of employers.
- It is important to maintain up-to-date knowledge of changes to VAT and payroll legislation and practice.
- Tax advisers regularly face ethical dilemmas in the course of their work, and threats to the fundamental ethical principles must be mitigated with appropriate safeguards.

## Activity answers

### Activity 1: Jim – VAT error

The correct answer is:

| | ✓ |
|---|---|
| Ignore the error as it is less than 1% of the box 6 figure for the quarter ended 31 March 2025. | |
| Add £450 to the box 1 figure for the VAT return for the quarter ended 30 June 2025. | |
| Deduct £450 from the box 1 figure for the VAT return for the quarter ended 30 June 2025. | ✓ |
| Obtain and complete form VAT652 'Notification of Errors in VAT Returns'. | |

A is wrong as an error should never be ignored; the 1% threshold applies to whether the error can be rectified on the return or should be notified separately, not to whether the error should be corrected at all. B would duplicate the error and D is not required as the error is less than £10,000, which itself is greater than 1% of the box 6 figure (ie £40).

### Activity 2: X Ltd error

The correct answer is:

| | ✓ |
|---|---|
| A correction can be made on the next VAT return as the error is less than 1% of turnover. | |
| A correction cannot be made on the next return as the error exceeds £10,000. | |
| A correction cannot be made on the next return as the error exceeds £50,000. | ✓ |

The error is less than 1% of turnover, but that is subject to an overall limit of £50,000.

### Activity 3: Late VAT returns

The correct answer is:

| | ✓ |
|---|---|
| 0 | |
| 2 | |
| 3 | ✓ |
| 4 | |

The VAT returns for the quarters ended 31 March 2025 and 30 June 2025 are both late (due 7 May and 7 August respectively), so with two failures at 8 August 2025, the business has 2 points.

The VAT return for the quarter ended 30 September 2025 is on time.

The VAT return for the quarter ended 31 December 2025 is late (it was due on 7 February 2026. So far the business has accumulated 3 points. None of them have expired as they were all given within the last two years.

No further failures have occurred in 2026 as all returns are submitted on time, so the balance on 8 February 2027 is 3.

The very first penalty point given for the quarter ended 31 March 2025 will expire on 31 May 2027.

### Activity 4: Late payment of VAT

Answer to the nearest pound.

The penalty for late payment in respect of the quarter ended 31 March 2025 is £ 0

The penalty for late payment in respect of the quarter ended 30 June 2025 is £ 960

The penalty for late payment in respect of the quarter ended 30 September 2025 is £ 966

The penalty is £0 for the quarter ended 31 March 2025 because it is paid within 15 days of its due date.

The penalty is £960 for the quarter ended 30 June 2025 being 3% of the balance outstanding at the end of day 15. The tax is paid in full before it is 30 days late so no further penalty is due for this quarter's late payment.

The penalty for the quarter ended 30 September 2025 is £966.

| | | |
|---|---|---|
| Up to 15 days late | 3% × £15,000 | 450 |
| 16-30 days late | 3% × £15,000 | 450 |
| Over 30 days late | 16/365 × 10% × £15,000 | 66 |
| Total | | 966 |

### Activity 5: Ian Morris – Client communication

To: Ian Morris

From: Mr Shelton

Date: 30 December

Subject: Change of VAT rate

Dear Ian Morris,

Further to your recent email, I have set out below the options open to you in relation to the standard rate of VAT.

Until recently, you have been charging VAT at a rate of (1) 20% . Therefore, a VAT-exclusive sale with a value of £1,000 has cost your non-registered clients (2) £ 1,200 .

The two options open to you are as follows:

- Keep the same VAT-exclusive value of £1,000.

The benefit of this option is that you have the same amount of VAT-exclusive sales value per item sold. However, this will now make the VAT-inclusive cost to your customers higher at (3) £ 1,250 . This may make your prices less competitive (if your competitors do not do the same) and may result in a loss of some customers.

- Keep the same VAT-inclusive value of (4) £ 1,200 .

Under this alternative option, you will remain competitive to your customers. However, your VAT-exclusive sales value per item sold will be reduced to (5) £ 960 .

There is no obvious correct option to choose; it will depend primarily on the strength of your competitors.

If you wish to discuss this with me in more detail, please do not hesitate to contact me.

Yours sincerely,

Mr Shelton

*Working*

£1,200 × 100/125 = £960

### Activity 6: Fundamental principles

The correct answers are:

| | ✓ |
|---|---|
| Integrity | ✓ |
| Objectivity | ✓ |
| Professional competence and due care | |
| Confidentiality | |
| Professional behaviour | ✓ |

Integrity: It would not be honest to knowingly reclaim an excessive amount of input tax.

Objectivity: Agreeing to the Finance Director's request because of the impact on job prospects would be to allow bias to affect judgement.

Professional behaviour: Submitting a tax return that does not follow tax law is illegal.

# Test your learning

1 **Identify which one of the following statements is correct.**

| | ✓ |
|---|---|
| If a net error of more than the lower of £10,000 and 1% of turnover (subject to an overall £5,000 limit) is discovered, it must be disclosed on form VAT652. | |
| If a net error of more than the greater of £10,000 and 1% of turnover (subject to an overall £5,000 limit) is discovered, it must be disclosed on form VAT652. | |
| If a net error of more than the lower of £10,000 and 1% of turnover (subject to an overall £50,000 limit) is discovered, it must be disclosed on form VAT652. | |
| If a net error of more than the greater of £10,000 and 1% of turnover (subject to an overall £50,000 limit) is discovered it must be disclosed on form VAT652. | |

2 **Identify whether the following statement is true or false.**

| | True ✓ | False ✓ |
|---|---|---|
| Tax avoidance is illegal and could lead to fines and/or imprisonment. | | |

3 You are a trainee accounting technician working for a sole trader, Mr Smith. Mr Smith has just received a letter from a client, Michael James (a trader making only standard-rated supplies to non-VAT-registered clients), asking about the impact of a recent change in the standard rate of VAT on his clients. The rate changed from 20% to 18%. He is undecided about whether to change his prices.

**Required**

**You are required to complete the following letter to Michael James, discussing the options open to him.**

Mr Smith

Number Street

London

SW11 8AB

Mr James

Alphabet Street

London

W12 6WM

Dear Mr James

CHANGE IN THE STANDARD RATE OF VAT

Further to your recent letter, I have set out below the options open to you in relation to the standard rate of VAT.

Until recently, you have been charging VAT at a rate of (1) [(1) ▼]. Therefore, a VAT-exclusive sale with a value of £1,000 has cost your non-VAT-registered clients (2) £ [(2) ▼] (£1,000 plus VAT).

The two options open to you are as follows:

- Keep the same VAT-exclusive value of £1,000.

Under this option, you would have the same amount of VAT-exclusive sales value per item sold.

However, this will now make the VAT-inclusive cost to your customers lower at (3) [(3) ▼]. You have effectively passed on the VAT saving to your customers.

- Keep the same VAT-inclusive value of (4) £ [(4) ▼].

Under this alternative option, you are not passing the VAT saving to your customers, which they may query, especially if your competitors reduce their prices. However, the benefit of this option is that your VAT-exclusive sales value per item sold will be increased to (5) [(5) ▼].

There is no obvious correct option to choose; it will depend primarily on the actions of your competitors.

If you wish to discuss this with me in more detail, please do not hesitate to contact me.

Yours sincerely

Mr Smith

**Picklist 1**

- 10%
- 20%
- 25%

**Picklist 2**

- 1,000
- 1,200
- 1,250

**Picklist 3**

- £1,000
- £1,180 (£1,000 plus VAT at 18%)

**Picklist 4**

- 1,000
- 1,180
- 1,200

**Picklist 5**

- £1,000 (£1,200 × 100/120)
- £1,016.95 (£1,200 × 100/118)

4 A taxpayer should try and resolve a VAT query in the following order.

**Required**

**Fill in the blank space from the picklist below.**

A taxpayer should try and resolve a VAT query in the following order:

| | |
|---|---|
| Firstly... | ▼ |
| If no luck, then... | ▼ |
| Still cannot resolve, then... | ▼ |

**Picklist**

- Check HMRC website.
- Ring the HMRC VAT helpline.
- Write to or email HMRC.

5 **Identify which one of the following statements is correct.**

| | ✓ |
|---|---|
| A VAT officer will usually turn up for a control visit unannounced. | |
| A VAT officer can check the correct amount of VAT has been paid or reclaimed. | |
| A VAT officer is not entitled to examine the business records. | |

6 A business made a 'small' overstatement of input tax on a previous return.

**Required**

**What effect will this have on the current VAT payable to HMRC?**

| | ✓ |
|---|---|
| An increase in the VAT payable via the current return. | |
| A decrease in the VAT payable via the current return. | |
| No impact on the current return. It must simply be separately declared. | |

7 A business made a 'small' understatement of output tax on a previous return.

**Required**

**Should this adjustment be shown on the latest VAT return, and if so, where on the return?**

| | ✓ |
|---|---|
| No – not shown on the return | |
| Yes – shown in box 1 | |
| Yes – shown in box 4 | |

8 A business pays their PAYE tax liabilities as follows for the tax year 2025/26:

| Tax month ended | Amount<br>£ | On time/late |
|---|---|---|
| 5 May 2025 | 20,000 | Late |
| 5 June 2025 | 22,000 | On time |
| 5 July 2025 | 22,000 | Late |
| 5 August 2025 | 23,500 | Late |
| 5 September 2025 | 24,200 | On time |
| 5 October 2025 | 20,000 | Late |
| 5 November 2025 | 30,000 | On time |
| 5 December 2025 | 28,000 | Late |
| 5 January 2026 | 18,000 | Late |
| 5 February 2026 | 21,000 | On time |
| 5 March 2026 | 25,000 | Late |
| 5 April 2026 | 26,000 | Late |

None of the late payments were over 6 months overdue.

**Required**

**What total late payment of PAYE penalties will apply to the business in respect of 2025/26?**

£ [ ]

**VAT account**

| Date<br>20XX | Reference | Debit<br>£ | Date<br>20XX | Reference | Credit<br>£ |
|---|---|---|---|---|---|
| 1.1–31.3 | Sales returns day book | 474.80 | 1.1–31.3 | Sales day book | 10,422.20 |
| 1.1–31.3 | Purchases day book | 3,596.00 | 1.1–31.3 | Cash book – UK sales | 2,069.00 |
| 31.3 | Bad debt relief | 195.00 | 1.1–31.3 | Purchases returns day book – UK purchases | 204.00 |
| 31.3 | VAT reclaimed on imports (postponed accounting) | 651.20 | 31.3 | Fuel scale charge | 28.83 |
| 31.3 | Balance b/d | 8,458.23 | 31.3 | VAT on imports (postponed accounting) | 651.20 |
| | **Total** | **13,375.23** | | **Total** | **13,375.23** |

| Date 20XX | Reference | Debit £ | Date 20XX | Reference | Credit £ |
|---|---|---|---|---|---|
| | | | | VAT payable | 8,458.23 |

**Required**

**Use the above VAT account to complete the email below.**

To: Finance Director

From: Accounting Technician

Date: 25 April 20XX

Subject: VAT return to 31 March 20XX

Please be advised that I have now completed the VAT return for the quarter to 31 March 20XX. If you are in agreement with the figures shown in the return, please could you arrange an electronic payment of £[ ] to be made by [ ▼ ].

If you wish to discuss this further, please feel free to call me.

Kind regards

**Picklist**

- 30 April 20XX
- 7 June 20XX
- 7 May 20XX

10 Doug is a retailer and has been selling goods to the general public for £235 (VAT inclusive) while the VAT rate was 17.5% (VAT fraction 7/47). When the VAT rate changed to 20% he did not want to change the cost of these goods to his customers who are not VAT-registered.

**Required**

**Work out for Doug the VAT-exclusive amount of the goods sold both before and after the change in the VAT rate.**

| VAT inclusive £ | VAT rate | VAT exclusive £ |
|---|---|---|
| 235.00 | 17.5% | |
| 235.00 | 20% | |

# Test your learning answers

## Chapter 1

1 The correct answer is:

| | |
|---|---|
| HM Customs & Excise | |
| Inland Revenue | |
| HM Revenue & Customs | ✓ |
| HM Treasury | |

2 The correct answer is:

| | |
|---|---|
| Output VAT is the VAT charged by a supplier on the sales that are made by their business. Output VAT is collected by the supplier and paid over to HMRC. | ✓ |
| Output VAT is the VAT suffered by the purchaser of the goods which will be reclaimed from HMRC if the purchaser is VAT-registered. | |

The other statement describes input VAT.

3 VAT is collected by HMRC throughout the manufacturing/supply chain for goods. Each VAT-registered business that buys, processes and then sells the goods pays the difference between the VAT on their sale and the VAT on their purchase over to HMRC.

---

## Chapter 2

1 The correct answers are:

| | True ✓ | False ✓ |
|---|---|---|
| If a business supplies zero-rated services, then the business is not able to reclaim the VAT on its purchases and expenses from HMRC. | | ✓ |
| A business makes zero-rated supplies. The cost to the business of its purchases and expenses is the VAT-exclusive amount. | ✓ | |

2 AN Accountant

Number Street

London

SW11 8AB

Mrs Quirke

Alphabet Street

London

W12 6WM

Dear Mrs Quirke

VAT REGISTRATION

Further to our recent telephone conversation, set out below are the circumstances when you must register your business for VAT.

If the taxable turnover of your business at the end of a month, looking back no more than [12] months, has exceeded the registration limit of [£90,000], then the business must apply to register for VAT within 30 days.

Alternatively, if at any time, the taxable turnover (before any VAT is added) is expected to exceed the registration limit within the next [30 days] alone, then the business must apply to be registered for VAT without delay. This would be the situation if, for example, you obtained a large additional contract for, say, £92,000.

If you wish to discuss this in any more detail, please do not hesitate to contact me.

Yours sincerely

AN Accountant

**3** By what date will Amy exceed the threshold for VAT? [30 April 2026]

By what date must Amy register for VAT? [30 May 2026]

VAT registration is required when taxable supplies (standard plus zero-rated supplies) exceed £90,000. Taxable supplies are £10,060 (£7,850 + £2,210) per month.

Amy exceeds this threshold after nine months, ie by 30 April 2026, as taxable supplies are then £90,540 (9 × £10,060).

**4** The correct answer is:

| | |
|---|---|
| At the beginning of month 12, Richard expects his taxable supplies to exceed £90,000 in the next 30 days. | |
| At the end of month 12, Richard's taxable supplies in the previous 12 months will have exceeded £90,000. | ✓ |

The historic test is met at the end of month 12.

For the future test to be met, the taxable supplies in the next 30 days **alone** must exceed the threshold, ie the taxable supplies in the previous 11 months are not included. Therefore, the future test is not met here.

**5** The correct answer is:

| | |
|---|---|
| Preparation of VAT returns would be optional. | |
| Customers would benefit by being able to claim back input tax. | |
| It is a new business and wishes to appear larger or more established. | ✓ |

Once registered, even voluntarily, VAT returns will have to be completed.

VAT-registered customers would neither gain nor lose because they could reclaim VAT charged to them, and non-VAT-registered customers would be disadvantaged because they would be charged VAT they could not reclaim.

6 Freya must notify HMRC that she is liable to register for VAT by 10/05/2025, and her registration will take effect on 10/04/2025.

The historic test does not trigger compulsory registration as Freya's supplies in the last 12 months to 31/03/X5 is (12 × £6,000) = £72,000. However, on 10/04/X5 she exceeds the registration limit of £90,000 in the next 30 days alone. She has until the end of the 30 day period to notify HMRC and her registration takes effect immediately.

---

## Chapter 3

1 **(a)** The VAT is £ 76.80

VAT = £384.00 × 20%

= £76.80

**(b)** The correct answers are:

| | Output tax ✓ | Input tax ✓ |
|---|---|---|
| Business C | ✓ | |
| Business D | | ✓ |

2 The correct answers are:

| | ✓ |
|---|---|
| Staff party | |
| Car for sales manager | ✓ |
| Photocopier | |
| Entertaining UK clients | ✓ |

3

| VAT inclusive £ | VAT at 20% £ |
|---|---|
| 42.88 | 7.14 |
| 96.57 | 16.09 |
| 28.20 | 4.70 |
| 81.07 | 13.51 |

*Working*

(1) £42.88 × 1/6 = £7.14

(2) £96.57 × 1/6 = £16.09

(3) £28.20 × 1/6 = £4.70

(4) £81.07 × 1/6 = £13.51

4 The correct answer is:

| | ✓ |
|---|---|
| The goods will be treated as standard-rated in the UK if the US-based business is VAT-registered. | |
| The goods will be treated as standard-rated in the UK, provided documentary evidence of the export is obtained within three months. | |
| The goods will be treated as zero-rated in the UK if the US-based business is VAT-registered. | |
| The goods will be treated as zero-rated in the UK, provided documentary evidence of the export is obtained within three months. | ✓ |

5

| Net<br>£ | VAT rate<br>% | VAT<br>£ | Gross<br>£ |
|---|---|---|---|
| 43.50 | 20 | 8.70 | 52.20 |
| 18.00 | 20 | 3.60 | 21.60 |

*Workings*

1 VAT = £52.20 × 1/6
= £8.70

2 VAT = £18.00 × 20%
= £3.60

6 The correct answers are:

| | True ✓ | False ✓ |
|---|---|---|
| A VAT-registered business can reclaim all the input tax attributed to zero-rated supplies. | ✓ | |
| A VAT-registered business can reclaim all the input tax attributed to standard-rated supplies. | ✓ | |
| A VAT-registered business can reclaim all the input tax attributed to exempt supplies. | | ✓ |
| A VAT-registered business can reclaim all the input tax attributed to both taxable and exempt supplies providing certain tests are satisfied. | ✓ | |

7 The correct answer is:

| | ✓ |
|---|---|
| No VAT is charged by the overseas supplier; therefore this can be ignored by Joe on his VAT return. | |
| Joe must pay output tax to HMRC at the port/airport and can reclaim input tax on the next return. | |
| Joe must charge himself 'output tax' and reclaim 'input tax' on the same return. | ✓ |

## Chapter 4

1 The correct answer is:

| | ✓ |
|---|---|
| 1 year | |
| 2 years | |
| 6 years | ✓ |
| 20 years | |

2 The correct answers are:

| | ✓ |
|---|---|
| The invoice must clearly state that a domestic reverse charge applies. | ✓ |
| The invoice must include VAT at the reduced rate of 5%. | |
| The customer is unable to recover any input tax in relation to such invoices. | |
| The customer is obliged to include the correct VAT on the invoice as output tax on their own VAT return. | ✓ |

3

| | Date | Basic (B)/ Actual (A) |
|---|---|---|
| An invoice is sent out to a customer for goods on 22 June 2025 and the goods are despatched on 29 June 2025. | 22 June | A |
| Goods are sent out to a customer on 18 June 2025 and this is followed by an invoice on 23 June 2025. | 23 June | A |
| A customer pays in full for goods on 27 June 2025 and they are then delivered to the customer on 2 July 2025. | 27 June | A |

4 The correct answer is:

| | ✓ |
|---|---|
| 15 May 2025 | |
| 20 May 2025 | ✓ |
| 20 June 2025 | |

The earliest date is the despatch on 15 May. As the invoice is sent within 14 days, the invoice date becomes the tax point.

5 The correct answers are:

| | ✓ |
|---|---|
| 2 June 2025 | ✓ |
| 11 June 2025 | ✓ |
| 29 June 2025 | |
| 31 July 2025 | |

**Deposit**

The cash paid for the deposit is the earliest date so 2 June is the tax point for the deposit.

**Balance**

Despatch is the earliest date relating to the balancing payment. This is not overridden by the invoice date as the invoice is sent more than 14 days later. So the despatch date of 11 June is the tax point for the balancing payment.

6 The VAT on a bad debt can be reclaimed from HMRC when the following conditions are met:

- The debt is more than six months overdue and less than four years and six months old.
- The original VAT on the invoice has been paid to HMRC.
- The debt is written-off in the accounts of the business.

---

## Chapter 5

1 The correct answers are:

| | True ✓ | False ✓ |
|---|---|---|
| If input VAT is greater than output VAT on the return, VAT is payable to HMRC. | | ✓ |
| If output VAT is greater than input VAT on the return, VAT is repayable from HMRC. | | ✓ |

If input VAT is greater than output VAT on the return, then VAT is repayable, and if output VAT is greater than input VAT on the return, then VAT is payable to HMRC.

2 The correct answer is:

| | ✓ |
|---|---|
| The payment of £4,700 for the previous quarter has been included twice in the VAT account. | |
| The payment of £4,700 for the previous quarter has been omitted from the VAT account. | ✓ |

By omitting the VAT paid debit of £4,700, the balance on the account is showing as £12,220 instead of the correct £7,520.

| Date 20XX | Reference | Debit £ | Date 20XX | Reference | Credit £ |
|---|---|---|---|---|---|
| QTR 1 | VAT paid | | QTR 1 | VAT payable | 4,700.00 |
| | | | QTR 2 | VAT payable | 7,520.00 |
| | Balance | 12,220.00 | | | |
| | **Total** | **12,220.00** | | **Total** | **12,220.00** |
| | | | QTR 2 | VAT payable | 12,220.00 |

3 The correct answers are:

| | ✓ |
|---|---|
| Sales (net of sales returns), totalling £19,314 | |
| Purchases returns £400 | |
| VAT on sales returns £79.77 | |
| VAT on credit purchases £2,090.17 | ✓ |
| VAT on cash purchases £606.60 | ✓ |
| Irrecoverable debts expense £192.00 | |
| VAT on irrecoverable debts £38.40 | ✓ |
| VAT on purchases returns (£80.00) | ✓ |

4 The correct answer is:

| | ✓ |
|---|---|
| Input tax paid at the ports is reclaimed as input tax on the VAT return. | |
| Both input tax and output tax in relation to the goods are shown on the VAT return. | ✓ |
| They are zero-rated and so no VAT features on the VAT return. | |
| They are exempt and so no VAT features on the VAT return. | |

5 The correct answers are:

| | ✓ |
|---|---|
| The fuel scale charge decreases input VAT and is shown in box 4. | |
| VAT on purchases of services from overseas increases both input VAT and output VAT and is shown in boxes 1 and 4. | ✓ |
| VAT on credit notes received from suppliers reduces input VAT and is shown in box 4. | ✓ |
| Credit notes issued to customers reduce sales and are shown in box 7. | |

Sales and other outputs, reduced by credit notes issued to customers, are shown in Box 6, not box 7.

6

| VAT return for quarter ended 31.03.2025 | | £ |
|---|---|---|
| VAT due in this period on **sales** and other outputs | Box 1 | 2,080.00 |
| Total value of **sales** and all other outputs, excluding any VAT. **Include your box 8 figure. Whole pounds only** | Box 6 | 18,450 |

*Working*

Box 1 = (7,200 + 3,200) × 20%

Box 6 = 7,200 + 2,705 + 5,345 + 3,200

7 The correct answers are:

| | ✓ |
|---|---|
| Box 1 | ✓ |
| Box 4 | ✓ |
| Box 6 | |
| Box 7 | ✓ |

## Chapter 6

1

AN Accountant

Number Street

London

SW11 8AB

Mr Lymstock

Alphabet Street

London

W12 6WM

Dear Mr Lymstock

ANNUAL ACCOUNTING SCHEME

I have recently been reviewing your files. I would like to make you aware of a scheme that you could use for VAT.

As the annual value of your taxable supplies, [excluding] VAT, in the following 12 months is expected to be [no more than] [£1,350,000] you can join the annual accounting scheme.

Under this scheme, you usually make [9] monthly direct debit payments based on your VAT liability for the previous year. The first of these payments is due at the end of the [fourth] month of the accounting period. You must then prepare a VAT return for the year and submit it with the balancing payment by [two months] after the year end.

Use of this annual accounting scheme is a great help, as it means that you only have to prepare [1] VAT return each year.

If you wish to discuss this with me in more detail, please do not hesitate to contact me.

Yours sincerely

AN Accountant

2 If the annual value of taxable supplies, [excluding] VAT, is [no more than] [£1,350,000], provided that a trader has a clean record with HMRC, he may be able to apply to use the cash accounting scheme.

The scheme allows the accounting for VAT to be based on the date of [receipt and payment of money]. This is particularly useful for a business which gives its customers a [long] period of credit while paying its suppliers promptly.

The scheme also gives automatic relief [for bad debts], so if the customer does not pay the amount due, then the VAT need not be accounted for to HMRC.

3 **(a)** The correct answer is:

| | ✓ |
|---|---|
| £897.00 | |
| £1,092.50 | |
| £1,311.00 | ✓ |

*Working*

£9,500 × 120% × 11.5% = £1,311.00

**(b)** The correct answer is:

| | ✓ |
|---|---|
| More VAT is payable not using the flat rate scheme. | |
| More VAT is payable using the flat rate scheme. | ✓ |

*Working*

If not using the flat rate scheme, the VAT payable would be:

| | | £ |
|---|---|---|
| Output tax | £9,500 × 20% | 1,900.00 |
| Input tax | £3,000 × 20% | (600.00) |
| | | 1,300.00 |

**4** The correct answers are:

| | True ✓ | False ✓ |
|---|---|---|
| The first payment due to HMRC is by 1 April 2025. | | ✓ |

The first payment due to HMRC is by 30 April 2025 (ie the **end** of month 4).

**5** The correct answer is:

| | ✓ |
|---|---|
| Yes, because they would be able to reclaim input VAT earlier. | |
| Yes, because they would pay output VAT later. | |
| No, because they would reclaim input VAT later. | ✓ |
| No, because they would pay output VAT earlier. | |

**6** The correct answer is:

| | ✓ |
|---|---|
| £2,550 | |
| £3,060 | |
| £2,010 | |
| £2,260 | ✓ |

The VAT due to HMRC is 8.5% of the VAT-inclusive figure, less the input VAT on fixed assets costing over £2,000.

(£30,000 × 120%) × 8.5% – (£4,800 × 20/120) = £2,260

## Chapter 7

1 £1,913.34

*Working*

| | Amount<br>£ |
|---|---|
| Gross pay (£27,000/12) | 2,250.00 |
| Income tax | (240.50) |
| Employee's NIC | (96.16) |
| Net pay | 1,913.34 |

2 The correct answers are:

| | Statutory deduction<br>✓ | Voluntary deduction<br>✓ |
|---|---|---|
| Student loan repayments | ✓ | |
| Income tax | ✓ | |
| Employee's NIC | ✓ | |
| Trade union fees | | ✓ |

3 The correct answers are:

| | True<br>✓ | False<br>✓ |
|---|---|---|
| Employer's NIC are deducted from gross pay | | ✓ |
| Employer's pension contributions are in addition to gross pay | ✓ | |

4 The correct answers are:

| | ✓ |
|---|---|
| The previous tax year's FPS forms | ✓ |
| Records of PAYE deducted from an employee who retired 12 months ago | ✓ |
| Payroll giving documents from 6 years ago | |
| Current employees' next of kin details | |
| Last year's business mileage claims made by employees | ✓ |
| Number of days' sick leave per employee in the previous tax year | ✓ |

5

| | Picklist |
|---|---|
| FPS | Whenever an employee is paid |
| EPS | Monthly (if required) |
| P60 | Annually |
| P45 | Whenever an employee leaves |
| P11D | Annually |
| Payslip | Whenever an employee is paid |

6

- The amounts of each deduction that is variable in nature, eg income tax and NIC
- The number of hours worked, as the employee is paid an hourly rate

7 **(a)** Form giving details of taxable earnings and tax deducted for the tax year ended 5 April 2026 – P60, receivable by 31 May 2026.

**(b)** Form giving details of benefits for the tax year ended 5 April 2026 – P11D, receivable by 6 July 2026.

## Chapter 8

1 The correct answer is:

| | ✓ |
|---|---|
| If a net error of more than the lower of £10,000 and 1% of turnover (subject to an overall £5,000 limit) is discovered, it must be disclosed on form VAT652. | |
| If a net error of more than the greater of £10,000 and 1% of turnover (subject to an overall £5,000 limit) is discovered, it must be disclosed on form VAT652. | |
| If a net error of more than the lower of £10,000 and 1% of turnover (subject to an overall £50,000 limit) is discovered, it must be disclosed on form VAT652. | |
| If a net error of more than the greater of £10,000 and 1% of turnover (subject to an overall £50,000 limit) is discovered it must be disclosed on form VAT652. | ✓ |

2 The correct answers are:

| | True ✓ | False ✓ |
|---|---|---|
| Tax avoidance is illegal and could lead to fines and/or imprisonment. | | ✓ |

Tax **evasion** is illegal and could lead to fines and/or imprisonment, as opposed to tax **avoidance**.

3 Mr Smith

Number Street

London

SW11 8AB

Mr James

Alphabet Street

London

W12 6WM

Dear Mr James

CHANGE IN THE STANDARD RATE OF VAT

Further to your recent letter, I have set out below the options open to you in relation to the standard rate of VAT.

Until recently, you have been charging VAT at a rate of (1) [20%]. Therefore, a VAT-exclusive sale with a value of £1,000 has cost your non-VAT-registered clients (2) £ [1,200] (£1,000 plus VAT).

The two options open to you are as follows:

- Keep the same VAT-exclusive value of £1,000.

Under this option, you would have the same amount of VAT-exclusive sales value per item sold. However, this will now make the VAT-inclusive cost to your customers lower at (3) [£1,180 (£1,000 plus VAT at 18%)]. You have effectively passed on the VAT saving to your customers.

- Keep the same VAT-inclusive value of (4) £ [1,200].

Under this alternative option, you are not passing the VAT saving to your customers, which they may query, especially if your competitors reduce their prices. However, the benefit of this option is that your VAT-exclusive sales value per item sold will be increased to (5) [£1,016.95 (£1,200 × 100/118)].

There is no obvious correct option to choose; it will depend primarily on the actions of your competitors.

If you wish to discuss this with me in more detail, please do not hesitate to contact me.

Yours sincerely

Mr Smith

4 A taxpayer should try and resolve a VAT query in the following order:

| | |
|---|---|
| Firstly... | check HMRC website. |
| If no luck, then... | ring the HMRC VAT helpline. |
| Still cannot resolve, then... | write to or email HMRC. |

**5** The correct answer is:

| | ✓ |
|---|---|
| A VAT officer will usually turn up for a control visit unannounced. | |
| A VAT officer can check the correct amount of VAT has been paid or reclaimed. | ✓ |
| A VAT officer is not entitled to examine the business records. | |

**6** The correct answer is:

| | ✓ |
|---|---|
| An increase in the VAT payable via the current return. | ✓ |
| A decrease in the VAT payable via the current return. | |
| No impact on the current return. It must simply be separately declared. | |

**7** The correct answer is:

| | ✓ |
|---|---|
| No – not shown on the return | |
| Yes – shown in box 1 | ✓ |
| Yes – shown in box 4 | |

It is shown as an increase in the output tax in box 1 on the VAT return.

**8** £ 2,855

There are 8 late payments in the tax year, ie 7 defaults (as the first late payment is ignored).

Defaults 1–3 (July, August and October): 1% x £(22,000 + 23,500 + 20,000) = £655

Defaults 4–6 (December, January and March): 2% x £(28,000 + 18,000 + 25,000) = £1,420

Default 7 (April): 3% x £26,000 = £780

Total penalties are therefore £2,855

**9** To: Finance Director

From: Accounting Technician

Date: 25 April 20XX

Subject: VAT return to 31 March 20XX

Please be advised that I have now completed the VAT return for the quarter to 31 March 20XX. If you are in agreement with the figures shown in the return, please could you arrange an electronic payment of £ 8,458.23 to be made by 7 May 20XX .

If you wish to discuss this further, please feel free to call me.

Kind regards

10

| VAT inclusive<br>£ | VAT rate | VAT exclusive<br>£ |
|---|---|---|
| 235.00 | 17.5% | 200.00 |
| 235.00 | 20% | 195.84 |

*Workings*

1 VAT rate of 17.5% (VAT fraction 7/47 or 17.5/117.5)

VAT-exclusive value £235 – (7/47 × £235) = £200

2 VAT rate of 20% (VAT fraction 1/6 or 20/120)

VAT-exclusive value £235 – (1/6 × £235) = £195.84

# Reference material for AAT assessment of Tax Processes for Businesses

## Introduction

This document comprises data that you may need to consult during your Tax Processes for Businesses computer-based assessment.

The material can be consulted during the sample and live assessments through pop-up windows. It is made available here so you can familiarise yourself with the content before the assessment.

Do not take a print of this document into the exam room with you*.

This document may be changed to reflect periodical updates in the computer-based assessment, so please check you have the most recent version while studying. This unit is based on Finance Act 2025 subject to assessment from 26 January 2026.

*Unless you need a printed version as part of reasonable adjustments for particular needs, in which case you must discuss this with your tutor at least six weeks before the assessment date.

# Contents

## 1 Rates of VAT

Taxable supplies:

| | |
|---|---|
| Standard rate | 20% |
| Reduced rate | 5% |
| Zero rate | 0% |

Non-taxable supplies have no VAT applied:

- Exempt
- Outside the scope of VAT

## 2 Registration and deregistration for VAT

| | |
|---|---|
| Registration threshold | £90,000 |
| Deregistration threshold | £88,000 |

| Compulsory registration | Notify HMRC | Registration effective from |
|---|---|---|
| Historic test | Within 30 days of the end of the month threshold was exceeded | First day of the second month after threshold exceeded |
| Future test | Before the end of the 30 day period that the threshold was expected to be exceeded | From the start of the 30 day period that the threshold was expected to be exceeded |

| Deregistration | Notify HMRC | Deregistration effective from |
|---|---|---|
| Compulsory | Within 30 days of the business ceasing to make taxable supplies | Date of cessation |
| Voluntary | Evidence that taxable supplies will not exceed the VAT deregistration threshold in the next 12 months | Date request received by HMRC, or agreed later date |

## 3 Failure to register for VAT

- This can result in a penalty for failure to notify. The penalty is a % of potential lost revenue (PLR):

| Type of behaviour | Within 12 months of tax being due | | 12 months or more after tax was due | |
|---|---|---|---|---|
| | unprompted | prompted | unprompted | prompted |
| Non-deliberate | 0–30% | 10–30% | 10–30% | 20–30% |
| Deliberate | 20–70% | 35–70% | 20–70% | 35–70% |
| Deliberate and concealed | 30–100% | 50–100% | 30–100% | 50–100% |

- Penalties will not be applied if there is a reasonable excuse.
- HMRC will treat the business as though it had registered on time and will expect VAT to be accounted for as if it had been charged. The business has two choices:
  - treat the invoices as VAT inclusive and absorb the VAT which should have been charged, or
  - account for VAT as an addition to the charges already invoiced and attempt to recover this VAT from its customers.

## 4 Changes to the VAT registration

HMRC must be notified of a change of:

| | |
|---|---|
| Name, trading name or address | Within 30 days |
| Partnership members | Within 30 days |
| Agent's details | Within 30 days |
| Bank account details | 14 days in advance. |
| Change in business activity | Within 30 days |

## 5 Keeping business and VAT records

| | |
|---|---|
| Record retention period | 6 years |
| Penalty for failure to keep records | £500 |

## 6 Contents of a VAT invoice

**Full VAT invoice**

- A sequential number based on one or more series which uniquely identifies the document
- The time of the supply (tax point)
- The date of issue of the document (where different to the time of supply)
- Supplier's name, address and VAT registration number
- Customer's name and address
- A description sufficient to identify the goods or services supplied
- For each description, the quantity of the goods or the extent of the services, the rate of VAT, and the amount payable excluding VAT – this can be expressed in any currency
- The gross total amount payable, excluding VAT – this can be expressed in any currency
- The rate of any cash discount offered
- The total amount of VAT chargeable – this must be expressed in sterling
- The unit price (applicable to countable elements)

**Simplified VAT invoices (≤£250)**

- Suppliers name, address and VAT registration number
- The time of supply (tax point)
- A description which identifies the goods or services supplied
- For each applicable VAT rate, the total amount payable, including VAT and the VAT rate

**Modified VAT invoices**

- A full VAT invoice showing the VAT inclusive rather than VAT exclusive values

## 7 Partial exemption for VAT

| | |
|---|---|
| De minimis amount | £625 per month |

| Proportion of total input VAT | ≤50% |
|---|---|

- Generally, partially exempt business cannot reclaim the input tax paid on purchases that relate to exempt supplies.
- If the amount of input tax incurred relating to exempt supplies is below a minimum de minimis amount, input tax can be reclaimed in full.
- If the amount of input tax incurred relating to exempt supplies is above the de minimis amount, only the part of the input tax that related to non-exempt supplies can be reclaimed.

## 8 International trade and VAT

| Export of goods | Zero-rated |
|---|---|
| Import of goods | UK VAT applied using Postponed accounting |
| Export of services | Apply UK VAT if place of supply is in the UK:<br>• For supplies to business, place of supply is the location of the customer (no UK VAT)<br>• For supplies to non-business customers, place of supply is the location of the supplier (charge UK VAT). |
| Import of services | Reverse charge applies |

## 9 Tax points for VAT

| Basic tax point date | Date of despatch of the goods/carrying out of the service |
|---|---|
| Actual tax point date may be earlier | If either:<br>• Payment is received earlier<br>• Invoice is issued earlier<br>Actual tax point becomes the earlier of these two dates. |
| Actual tax point date may be later | If:<br>• Invoice is issued within 14 days of despatch/ service (and advance payment didn't apply) |

- Deposits are treated separately to final payment and so may have a different tax point.
- The tax point is always the date of payment if cash basis is being applied.
- Where services are being supplied on a continuous basis over a period in excess of a month but invoices are being issued regularly throughout the period, a tax point is created every time an invoice is issued or a payment is made, whichever happens first.
- Goods on sale or return will have a tax point date either on adoption (the customer indicates they will keep the goods) or 12 months after removal of the goods where this is earlier.

## 10 Time limits for issuing a VAT invoice

- Within 30 days of tax point which is either:
  - within 30 days of date of supply or
  - within 30 days of payment if payment was in advance.

## 11 Blocked expenses and VAT

Input VAT cannot be recovered on blocked expenses.

**Business entertainment**

- The exception is that input tax can be reclaimed in respect of entertaining overseas customers, but not UK or Isle of Man customers.
- When the entertainment is in respect of a mixed group of both employees and non-employees (e.g. customers and/or suppliers), the business can only reclaim VAT on the proportion of the expenses that is for employees and on the proportion for overseas customers.

**Cars**

- Input VAT can only be recovered on cars if it is wholly for business (no private use).
- 50% of input VAT can be recovered when cars are hired/leased.
- VAT can be recovered on commercial vehicles such as vans/lorries.

**Assets with private use**

- The VAT recovery should be based only on the proportion related to business use.

## 12 Fuel scale charge and VAT

If the business pays for road fuel, it can deal with the VAT charged on the fuel in one of four ways:

- reclaim all of the VAT. All of the fuel must be used only for business purposes.
- reclaim all of the VAT and pay the appropriate fuel scale charge (see below) - this is a way of accounting for output tax on fuel that the business buys but that is then used for private motoring
- reclaim only the VAT that relates to fuel used for business mileage. Detailed records of business and private mileage must be kept
- do not reclaim any VAT. This can be a useful option if mileage is low and also if fuel is used for both business and private motoring. If the business chooses this option it must apply it to all vehicles, including commercial vehicles.
- The fuel scale charge is as follows:

| Description of vehicle: vehicle's $CO_2$ emissions figure | VAT inclusive consideration for a 12 month prescribed accounting period (£) | VAT inclusive consideration for a 3 month prescribed accounting period (£) | VAT inclusive consideration for a 1 month prescribed accounting period (£) |
|---|---|---|---|
| 120 or less | 661 | 164 | 54 |
| 125 | 990 | 248 | 82 |
| 130 | 1,059 | 263 | 87 |
| 135 | 1,122 | 280 | 93 |
| 140 | 1,191 | 297 | 99 |
| 145 | 1,255 | 313 | 103 |
| 150 | 1,323 | 330 | 109 |
| 155 | 1,387 | 347 | 115 |
| 160 | 1,456 | 363 | 120 |
| 165 | 1,520 | 380 | 126 |
| 170 | 1,588 | 396 | 131 |
| 175 | 1,652 | 412 | 137 |

| Description of vehicle: vehicle's CO2 emissions figure | VAT inclusive consideration for a 12 month prescribed accounting period (£) | VAT inclusive consideration for a 3 month prescribed accounting period (£) | VAT inclusive consideration for a 1 month prescribed accounting period (£) |
|---|---:|---:|---:|
| 180 | 1,721 | 429 | 143 |
| 185 | 1,784 | 446 | 148 |
| 190 | 1,853 | 462 | 153 |
| 195 | 1,917 | 479 | 159 |
| 200 | 1,985 | 496 | 164 |
| 205 | 2,049 | 512 | 170 |
| 210 | 2,118 | 528 | 175 |
| 215 | 2,182 | 545 | 181 |
| 220 | 2,250 | 561 | 187 |
| 225 or more | 2,314 | 578 | 192 |

- Where the CO2 emission figure is not a multiple of 5, the figure is rounded down to the next multiple of 5 to determine the level of the charge.

## 13 Bad debts and VAT

VAT that has been paid to HMRC and which has not been received from the customer can be reclaimed as bad debt relief. The conditions are that:

(a) the debt is more than six months and less than four years and six months old

(b) the debt has been written off in the VAT account and transferred to a separate bad debt account

(c) the debt has not been sold or handed to a factoring company

(d) the business did not charge more than the normal selling price for the items.

Bad debt relief does not apply when the cash accounting scheme is used because the VAT is not paid to HMRC until after the customer has paid it to the supplier.

## 14 Due dates for submitting the VAT return and paying electronically

| | |
|---|---|
| Deadline for submitting return and paying VAT–quarterly accounting | 1 months and 7 days after the end of the VAT period |
| Deadline if being paid by direct debit | HMRC will collect 3 working days after the submission deadline. |

- Please see alternative submission and payment deadlines for special accounting schemes.

## 15 Special accounting schemes for VAT

### 15.1 Annual accounting scheme for VAT

| | | |
|---|---|---|
| Joining the scheme | Maximum (estimated) taxable turnover in next 12 months | £1.35m |

| | | |
|---|---|---|
| Leaving the scheme | Compulsory if taxable turnover at the end of the VAT accounting year exceeds the threshold | £1.6m |
| VAT returns | One annual return | 2 months after the end of the accounting period |
| VAT payments (monthly) | Nine monthly interim payments (10% of estimated VAT bill based on previous returns) | At the end of months 4 to 12 in the accounting period. |
| | Balancing payment | 2 months after the end of the accounting period |
| VAT payments (quarterly) | Three interim payments (25% of estimated VAT bill based on previous returns) | At the end of months 4, 7 and 10 in the accounting period |
| | Balancing payment | 2 months after the end of the accounting period |

## 15.2 Cash accounting scheme for VAT

| | | |
|---|---|---|
| Joining the scheme | Maximum (estimated) taxable turnover in next 12 months | £1.35m |
| Leaving the scheme | Compulsory if taxable turnover at the end of the VAT accounting year exceeds the threshold | £1.6m |
| Deadlines for submission and payment | | Same as normal scheme |

## 15.3 Flat Rate Scheme for VAT

| | | |
|---|---|---|
| Joining the scheme | Maximum taxable turnover (excluding VAT) in the next 12 months | £150,000 |
| Leaving the scheme | On the anniversary of joining, maximum turnover in the last 12 months (including VAT) or expected turnover in next 12 months | £230,000 |
| Discount | In first year of being VAT-registered | 1% |
| Limited cost business | Goods cost less than either:<br>• 2% of turnover, or<br>• £1,000 a year | 16.5% |
| Capital expenditure | Input tax can be recovered on individual large capital purchases | £2,000 |

| Deadlines for submission and payment | | Same as normal scheme |
|---|---|---|

- The appropriate flat rate % will be provided in the assessment.

## 16 Errors in previous VAT Returns

Errors can be corrected that have been included in VAT returns for the preceding four years, as long as the net value of the errors is either:

- £10,000 or less
- between £10,000 and £50,000 but less than 1% of the total value of sales (Box 6).

For these kinds of errors, make an adjustment or correction in the next VAT return.

If VAT is due to HMRC because of the net errors, the net value of errors is added to the VAT due on sales and other outputs.

If VAT is reclaimable because of the net errors, the net value of errors is added to VAT reclaimed on purchases and other inputs.

HMRC must be informed separately about net errors that are:

- over £50,000
- over £10,000 if they exceed 1% of the total value of sales
- Deliberate errors

## 17 Late submission and late payment of VAT

**Late submission**

| Submission frequency | Penalty point threshold | Period of compliance |
|---|---|---|
| Annual | 2 points | 24 months |
| Quarterly | 4 points | 12 months |

| Initial penalty | £200 |
|---|---|
| Subsequent penalty | £200 |

| Removal of penalty points | |
|---|---|
| Business has not reached penalty threshold | Individual penalty points will expire automatically, depending on the date the VAT return was due.<br>If the deadline for the VAT return was:<br>• not the last day of a month – a penalty point expires on the last day of the month, 24 months after this; and<br>• the last day of a month – a penalty point expires on the last day of the month, 25 months after this. |
| Business has reached penalty threshold | All points will be reset to zero if both conditions below are met:<br>• a period of compliance (meeting all submission obligations on time for the period of compliance); and<br>• all submissions due in the preceding 24 months have been made (whether or not they were on time). |

Late payment

| Number of days overdue | First late payment penalty | Second late payment penalty |
|---|---|---|
| Up to 15 | None | None |
| 16 to 30 | 3% on the VAT outstanding at day 15 | None |
| 31 or more | 3% on the VAT outstanding at day 15<br>AND<br>3% on the VAT outstanding at day 30 | A daily rate based on 10% per annum charged every day from<br>day 31 until paid in full |

**Interest charged**

Interest is calculated at the Bank of England base rate plus 4%.

The Bank of England base rate will be given in the assessment.

## 18 Assessments of VAT

If a VAT Return is not submitted on time, HMRC will issue a 'VAT notice of assessment of tax' which will state how much HMRC think is owed.

If HMRC issue an assessment that is too low, a 30% penalty can be charged for not telling them it is incorrect within 30 days.

## 19 Penalties for inaccuracies in VAT return

A penalty can be charged as a percentage of the potential lost revenue (PLR):

| Type of behaviour | Unprompted disclosure<br>% | Prompted disclosure<br>% |
|---|---|---|
| Careless | 0-30 | 15-30 |
| Deliberate | 20-70 | 35-70 |
| Deliberate and concealed | 30-100 | 50-100 |

## 20 Payroll record retention

| Retention period | 3 years from end of tax year |
|---|---|
| Penalty for failure to maintain records | £3,000 |

## 21 Types of payroll submission

**Full Payment submission (FPS)**

- File on or before employees pay day.
- Include payments to and deductions for all employees.

**Employer payment summary (EPS)**

- File if no employees were paid in the month.
- Send by the 19th of the following tax month.

## 22 Payroll deadlines

| | |
|---|---|
| Registering for PAYE | You must register before the first payday.<br>You cannot register more than 2 months before you start paying people. |
| Month end date for PAYE | 5th of each month |
| Payment date for monthly payroll | 22nd of the following month if paid electronically.<br>19th otherwise.<br>If monthly amounts are <£1,500, quarterly payments can be made. |
| Provide employees with P60 | 31st May following the end of the tax year |
| Filing deadline for Expenses & Benefits forms | 6th July following the end of the tax year |
| Class 1A NIC payment date | 22nd July following the end of the tax year, if paying electronically.<br>19th July following the end of the tax year, otherwise. |

## 23 Penalties for late submission of payroll filings

Penalties may apply if:

- a FPS was late
- the expected amount of FPSs was not filed
- an EPS was not filed

| Number of employees | Monthly penalty |
|---|---|
| 1 to 9 | £100 |
| 10 to 49 | £200 |
| 50 to 249 | £300 |
| 250 or more | £400 |

Penalties may not apply if:

- The FPS is late but all reported payments on the FPS are within three days of the employees' payday (unless there is regular lateness).
- A new employer is late but sends the first FPS within 30 days of paying an employee.
- It is a business's first failure in the tax year to send a report on time.

## 24 Penalties for late payroll payment

**Late payment of monthly/quarterly payments**

- The first failure to pay in a tax year does not count as a default.
- Late payment penalties apply to late payments and payments of less than is due.

| Number of defaults in a tax year | Penalty percentage applied to the amount that is late in the relevant tax month |
|---|---|
| 1 to 3 | 1% |
| 4 to 6 | 2% |

| Number of defaults in a tax year | Penalty percentage applied to the amount that is late in the relevant tax month |
|---|---|
| 7 to 9 | 3% |
| 10 or more | 4% |

Additional penalties will apply if:

| | |
|---|---|
| A monthly or quarterly amount remains outstanding after 6 months | 5% of unpaid tax |
| A monthly or quarterly amount remains outstanding after 12 months | A further 5% of unpaid tax |

These additional penalties apply even where only one payment in the tax year is late.

**Late payments of amounts due annually or occasionally:**

| | |
|---|---|
| 30 days late | 5% |
| 6 months late | Additional 5% |
| 12 months late | Additional 5% |

**Interest**

Interest is calculated at the Bank of England base rate plus 4%.

The Bank of England base rate will be given in the assessment.

## 25 Penalties for inaccuracies in payroll returns

A penalty can be charged as a percentage of the potential lost revenue (PLR):

| Type of behaviour | Unprompted disclosure<br>% | Prompted disclosure<br>% |
|---|---|---|
| Careless | 0–30 | 15–30 |
| Deliberate | 20–70 | 35–70 |
| Deliberate and concealed | 30–100 | 50–100 |

# Glossary

## Chapter 1: Introduction to VAT

**Input VAT:** VAT on the purchase of goods and payment of expenses, which is reclaimed by the business from HMRC

**Output VAT :** VAT charged on the sale of goods and the provision of services by VAT-registered traders, which is paid by the business to HMRC

---

## Chapter 2: VAT basics

**Exempt supplies:** For example, insurance or postal services, are not taxable supplies, so no VAT is charged.

**Reduced-rated supplies:** Goods and services which are taxable at a rate of 5%, for example domestic fuel

**Registration:** The process required if a business making taxable supplies must (if it exceeds the registration limits), or wants to, start charging (and recovering) VAT. VAT must be charged on taxable supplies from the date of registration.

**Standard-rated supplies:** Goods and services which are taxable at a rate of 20%.

**Supplies outside the scope of VAT:** For example, wages; these are outside the UK VAT system altogether and have no impact on VAT calculations.

**Taxable supplies:** Taxable supplies are those which are:

- Standard-rated (20%)
- Zero-rated (0%)
- Reduced-rated (5%)

**Taxable turnover:** The VAT-exclusive value of all zero-rated, reduced-rated and standard-rated supplies. Exempt sales are excluded.

**Zero-rated supplies:** Goods and services which are taxable, but the rate of tax on them is 0%, for example non-luxury food, children's clothing

---

## Chapter 3: Inputs and outputs

**Fuel scale charge:** An output tax charge to offset against the input tax reclaimed on fuel purchased for private use.

**Partially exempt traders:** When a business makes a mixture of taxable and exempt supplies, input tax attributable to exempt supplies may only be reclaimed subject to satisfying *de minimis* tests.

---

## Chapter 4: Accounting for VAT

**Actual tax point:** A further date that can override the basic tax point if certain conditions are met.

**Bad debt relief:** A reclaim of output tax when a written-off debt is more than six months overdue.

**Basic tax point:** The date on which goods are despatched or services provided.

**Cash and petty cash payments book:** A record of all cash payments made by the business.

**Cash receipts book:** A record of all cash receipts of the business.

**Purchases day book:** A record of all invoices received from credit suppliers.

**Purchases returns day book:** A record of all credit notes received from credit suppliers.

**Sales day book:** A record of all invoices sent to credit customers.

**Sales returns day book:** A record of all credit notes sent to credit customers

**Simplified invoice:** An invoice that can be issued if the VAT-inclusive value of goods supplied is no more than £250.

**Tax point:** The date which determines when the VAT must be accounted for to HMRC

**VAT invoice:** A document that allows input tax to be claimed or output tax to be charged.

## Chapter 5: The VAT return

**Making Tax Digital:** The service businesses must use to keep digital records and submit their VAT returns.

**VAT (control) account:** The ledger account in which all amounts of input tax and output tax are recorded.

**VAT return:** The form which must be generated and submitted to HMRC to show the amount of VAT due or to be reclaimed, usually for the quarter.

## Chapter 6: VAT schemes for small businesses

**Annual accounting scheme:** A method of accounting for VAT which does not require quarterly returns and payments, but instead requires nine monthly direct debit payments and one annual return, accompanied by the final balancing payment.

**Cash accounting scheme:** A method of accounting for VAT which allows VAT to be dealt with according to the date of payment or receipt of cash, rather than under the normal tax point rules.

**Flat rate scheme:** Enables businesses to calculate their VAT payment as a percentage of total VAT-inclusive turnover.

## Chapter 7: Payroll systems

**Employer Payment Summary (EPS):** Month-end report reconciling FPSs to actual cash paid to employees and HMRC.

**Full Payment Submission (FPS):** Real-time report to HMRC of pay and deductions.

**Gross pay:** Total cash earnings for a pay period before any deductions.

**Net pay:** The net cash received by an employee after all deductions.

**Pay As You Earn (PAYE):** The system used for deducting tax from employees and reporting payroll information to HMRC.

**Taxable pay:** Amount on which income tax is due: earnings plus taxable benefits less allowable deductions.

## Chapter 8: VAT and PAYE Administration

**Error correction threshold:** This is the threshold that dictates whether errors discovered on a previous return can be corrected on the next return or must be reported separately.

**HMRC website:** The first place a taxpayer must check to try and resolve any VAT queries.

**Tax evasion:** Falsely reclaiming input tax/understating output tax or payroll taxes, obtaining bad debt relief or obtaining a repayment to which the business is not entitled.

# Index

## Tell us what you think

Got comments or feedback on this book? Let us know.
Use your QR code reader:

Or, visit:
**https://www.smartsurvey.co.uk/s/W30E6Y/**

### Need to get in touch with customer service?

www.bpp.com/request-support

### Spotted an error?

https://learningmedia.bpp.com/pages/errata